The Way of the S

Faeries are very real and powerful ⟨ dimension parallel to our own. These beings embody the enlightened energy of the elements, and the wisdom, energy, and primal force of creation. In this book you'll learn to work with the Sidhe, the faeries of the shining realm, to bridge polarities within your psyche, the world, and the universe.

Meet the great adepts of the Faerie Tradition, including Thomas the Rhymer, who traveled bodily into Faerieland. Learn how you can enter the Faerie realm and meet animal helpers and faerie allies that will help you realign with the natural world. Travel to the mystic cities of the Faerie realm to harmonize your inner and outer worlds. Then travel deeper into Faerieland and become an initiate of the Faerie Way to transform yourself from the spirit outward. Finally, tap the energy of the life-force itself and achieve ultimate wholeness when you merge with your "Co-Walker" in the Faerie world.

For Wiccans, the Faerie Way offers deep spiritual springs of renewal. For those on other paths, it provides a much-needed nondualistic, shamanic alternative to standard Western magical cosmology. The path into Faerieland lies open to everyone. If you're a seeker who longs to find "the land of heart's desire," *The Faerie Way* will guide your steps.

About the Author

Hugh Mynne was born in 1950 in Crosby, England. He graduated from the University College of North Wales with a B.A. Honours degree in religious studies. His early spiritual training was in the Japanese Zen tradition, and he obtained a preliminary "Kensho" (glimpse of reality) within this tradition.

Mr. Mynne currently lives in Ireland, where he gives seminars and workshops on shamanic techniques of healing, and coordinates a group studying the Faerie Tradition. He is married to the esoteric artist Eve Reid, and they share their cottage in County Derry with twenty-five cats.

To Write to the Author

If you wish to contact the author or would like more information about this book, please write to the author in care of Llewellyn Worldwide, and we will forward your request. Both the author and publisher appreciate hearing from you and learning of your enjoyment of this book. Llewellyn Worldwide cannot guarantee that every letter written to the author will be answered, but all will be forwarded. Please write to:

Hugh Mynne
%Llewellyn Worldwide
P.O. Box 64383, Dept. K483, St. Paul, MN 55164-0383, U.S.A.
Please enclose a self-addressed stamped envelope for reply, or $1.00 to cover costs.
If outside U.S.A., enclose international postal reply coupon.

Free Catalog from Llewellyn Worldwide

For more than 90 years, Llewellyn has brought its readers knowledge in the fields of metaphysics and human potential. Learn about the newest books in spiritual guidance, natural healing, astrology, occult philosophy, and more. Enjoy book reviews, new age articles, a calendar of events, plus current advertised products and services. To get your free copy of *Llewellyn's New Worlds of Mind and Spirit*, send your name and address to:

Llewellyn's New Worlds of Mind and Spirit
P.O. Box 64383 Dept. K483, St. Paul, MN 55164-0383, U.S.A.

Llewellyn's Celtic Wisdom Series

The Faerie Way

A Healing Journey to Other Worlds

Hugh Mynne

1998
Llewellyn Publications
St. Paul, MN 55164-0383, USA

FIRST EDITION
Second Printing, 1998

Cover design: Tom Grewe
Cover art: Nyease Merlin Somersett
Editor: Lisa Leonard
Book design and layout: Jessica Thoreson

Color illustrations by A.E. courtesy of the Ulster Museum, Belfast. Used by permission.

Acknowledgements and thanks are due to the following publishers and authors who have kindly granted permission to use illustrations and quotes from the following books:
HarperCollins Publishers Inc.: Selected excerpts from *The Spiral Dance*, Tenth Anniversary Edition, by Starhawk. Copyright © 1979, 1989, by Miriam Simos.
HarperCollins Publishers Inc.: *The Language of the Goddess* by Marija Gimbutas.
Bantam Press: *The Coming of the King* by Nikolai Tolstoy.
Penguin Books Ltd.: *The Myth of the Goddess* by Anne Baring and Jules Cashford.
Tsultrim Allione: *Women of Wisdom* by Tsultrim Allione (Penguin/ Arkana).
Thames and Hudson: *The Goddesses and Gods of Old Europe, 6500-3500 B.C.* by Marija Gimbutas.
Kindred Spirit Magazine: Interview with Arwyn Dreamwalker, *Kindred Spirit* No. 25 (*Kindred Spirit*, Foxhole, Dartington, Totnes, Devon TQ9 6EB England).
Souvenir Press: *Dimensions: A Casebook of Alien Contact* by Jacques Vallee.
ITP Routledge: *The Buddhist Teaching of Totality* by Garma C. C. Chang.

Cataloging-in-Publication Data
Mynne, Hugh.
    The faerie way: a healing journey to other worlds / Hugh Mynne. — 1st ed.
      p.   cm. — (Llewellyn's Celtic wisdom series)
    Includes bibliographical references (p.   ) and index.
    ISBN 1-56718-483-9 (pbk.)
    1. Fairies. 2. Spirits. 3. Celts—Religion. I. Title. II. Series.
    BF1552.M86   1996
    133.9—dc20   96-16408

Llewellyn Publications
A Division of Llewellyn Worldwide, Ltd.
P.O. Box 64383, Dept. K483, St. Paul, MN 55164-0383

Printed in the U.S.A.

About Llewellyn's Celtic Wisdom Series

Can it be said that we are all Celts? Certainly Western civilization owes as much, if not more, to our Celtic heritage as to Greek and Roman influences.

While the origins of the Celtic peoples are shrouded in the mists of time, they seem to have come from a civilization centered around Greece and the Aegean Sea in the third and fourth millennia B.C., moving out across Europe and occupying areas from Russia to Spain and finally, Scotland and Ireland in 1472 B.C.

The Celtic tribes were politically independent, and—in contrast to the Roman Empire—never truly united under a single ruler. That same independence brought Europeans to the New World, then pulled them westward across the continent through a need to create a "new order for the ages"—and a nation of people free of social, religious, political and economic oppression. Today, the same Celtic spirit asserts itself as people everywhere struggle for a new political reality.

Celtic art, music, magic and myth are unique, and are enjoying a renaissance today. Basic to the Celtic tradition is the acceptance of personal responsibility and realization that all of us constantly shape and affect the land on which we live. Intrinsic to this notion is the Celtic interrelationship with the Other-world and its inhabitants. The Celtic world view is a magical one, in which everything has a physical, mental and spiritual aspect and its own proper purpose, and where our every act affects both worlds.

The books of the Celtic Wisdom Series comprise a magical curriculum embracing ideas and techniques that awaken the soul to the myths and legends, the psychological and spiritual truths and the inner power each of us can tap to meet the challenges of our times.

To Caren, without whose help and loving assistance this book would not have been written; and in memory of Corona, Graham, Marg, Richard, Astaroth, Loki, Titania, Dickie, Pixie, and Max; also Kinker, beloved little feline member of the Family of Light who recently took the Path of the Stars. Happy Trails all.

Table of Contents

List of Illustrations

About the Color Plates

*Five faerie paintings by A.E., a great faerie seer, are reproduced within
this book as a stimulus to your own powers of inner vision.*

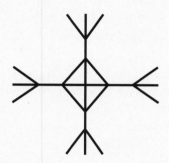

Reinventing the Tradition

A n old woman was sitting naked at the center of a magic circle. A small boy approached, fascinated. He was nine years old, and virtually blind as the result of an untreated eye condition. He could just make out the fuzzy outlines of the brass bowls filled with herbs around the circle's perimeter, and could smell their rich, deep, ancient aroma. It was as if a spring had been unsealed within him. He knew. He knew exactly what to do.

Removing his clothes, he joined the old woman in the circle. She was not much taller than he was. As he clung to her, wordless communication flashed between them. Her body seemed to grow enormous, throbbing with power. She was the Goddess, floating in black velvety space. Suddenly his vision cleared. He could see the innumerable diamond points of the stars. A deep ecstasy filled his being.

In a flash, the vision changed. The boy was in a jungle-like area,
green and lush, and a man was coming toward him. He could see green
moonlight flashing on the tines of his antlered head. This was the horned
god, powerful—awesomely powerful—and yet strangely, almost femi-
ninely, beautiful. Again the wordless communication flowed.

Soon, all too soon, he found himself back in the circle with the old
woman. She smiled strangely at him, and went on to show him the rit-
ual use of the herbs brimming in the brass bowls. Then she tenderly
washed him in butter, oil, and salt. When she had finished, he dressed
and returned home.

The boy in this story was Victor Anderson, who later went
on to cofound the Faerie Tradition of witchcraft. Understanding
the initiation experience described above is absolutely crucial to
the reopening of the Faerie Way in the twentieth century.
Although elements from the Alexandrian Book of Shadows later
entered the Faerie Tradition, the core Faerie vision—a view of
the universe totally unlike any other in modern occultism—persists today in the work of Anderson's successors. Its source may
well lie in Anderson's encounter with the old woman, who called
herself a faerie witch.

The Alexandrian connection enters the equation with
Gwydion Pendderwen. In the 1950s, Anderson and his wife broke
up a fight between their only son and a neighbor's boy. This boy
later changed his name to Gwydion Pendderwen and was initiated by the Andersons. Anderson and Pendderwen cofounded
the Faerie Tradition and together wrote most of its rituals.

It is known that Pendderwen once met with Alexandrian
witches during a trip to England, and that they probably shared
material from their Book of Shadows with him. However, it is the
non-Alexandrian elements in the Faerie Tradition which are of
concern to us.

These can best be displayed in a quotation from Starhawk's
book *The Spiral Dance* (published in 1979). In this book,
Starhawk (an initiate of Victor Anderson's Faerie Tradition)
speaks of the world-view of witchcraft as being based on a very
ancient insight indeed:

> *The mythology and cosmology of witchcraft are rooted in*
> *that "Paleolithic shaman's insight"—that all things are*

swirls of energy, vortexes of moving forces, currents in an
ever-changing sea. Underlying the appearance of separate-
ness, of fixed objects within a linear stream of time, reality
is a field of energies that congeal, temporarily, into forms.
In time, all "fixed" things dissolve only to coalesce again
into new forms, new vehicles.

The Alexandrian Tradition was based largely on the philosophy of the Qabalah and the Western/magickal Tradition, yet this
passage is based on entirely different assumptions. Indeed, its
implications strike deeply at one of the cardinal tenets of
Qabalah: the existence of fixed selves or "souls." It more closely
resembles, as I shall show, the world-view of Buddhism. The question is, was this core Faerie vision of the interdependence of all
living things the fruit of a genuinely ancient Western lineage?

Certainly, from this vision of wholeness remarkable things
flowed. Pendderwen founded two seminal organizations: Neme-
ton (a networking group formed in Oakland, California, in 1970)
and Forever Forests (a group to foster ecological consciousness
and sponsor annual tree plantings, formed in 1977). From the
very beginning, the Faerie vision seems to have been connected
to the increase of interest in ecological matters—not surprising
when you consider the implications of a philosophy of total interdependence. Pendderwen was also active in the pagan antinu-
clear movement, and was arrested along with members of
Starhawk's Reclaiming Collective at a demonstration at
Lawrence Livermore Laboratory in California in 1982.

The huge success of Starhawk's book *The Spiral Dance* must
also be considered. Perhaps more than any other work, this encap-
sulated the Faerie vision of the universe, and, for many readers,
also acted as a spur to action in defense of the environment.

This present work is an exploration of that vision, tracing it to
its deepest sources, both in the West and in the East. Ultimately,
however, "East" and "West" have no meaning, for the Faerie vision
derives from the deeper strata of universal human consciousness. In
the course of this exploration, much new information will be
revealed and a complete set of exercises will be given to enable the
reader to realize the vision in his or her own life. We begin in the
remote past with the people of Faerie themselves.

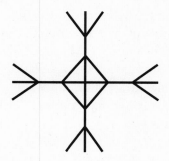

CHAPTER ONE

The Old Ways

For most people, the word "faerie" conjures up an instant mental picture—that of a diminutive winged sprite. This coy iconography is, as we shall see, quite misleading. The challenge is to break through the barrier it has created in the popular imagination.

One way to better understand this problem is to look at the roots of the word "faerie" and its Scottish/Irish equivalents *sith* and Sidhe. The scholarly consensus seems to be that faerie is derived primarily from three ancient words. The first of these is *fatum* or fate, referring to the goddesses (the Fatae) who ruled over or controlled human affairs. Second, there is a strong connection with the word *fatare*, meaning "to enchant." Third, and perhaps most important, there is a link with the Fatuae, a species of nymphs known in Latin mythology as "a race of immortal damsels." These Fatuae used to haunt places inaccessible to humans, such as remote waterfalls, lakes, woods, and fountains.

Lewis Spence refers to them succinctly as "spiritual maidens of the forests and elements."

By the time of the great medieval poets Chaucer, Gower, and Langland, the word "faerie" had acquired an augmented meaning. The Scottish poet Dunbar advises his readers, "evir be ready and addrest to pass out of this frawdfull fary" (i.e., the vain and ephemeral show of the world).

When we come to the Gaelic words *sith* and Sidhe, we find a similar range of meanings. In complete consonance with the derivation of the English word, J. MacDougall observes that *sithide* or *sith* is the genitive of *sithde*, "a female faerie" (*siochar* being the male form). Other meanings of *sith* or Sidhe include these: a hill or mound; divine, unearthly, supernatural; and Peace (the people of Peace being the faeries).

From the above we can more easily understand how faerie came to refer to a race of immortal (i.e., spiritual, supernatural), unseen female beings. Andrew Lang, in his Introduction to *Perrault's Fairy Tales*, refers to the term "good ladies" being popularly applied to the faeries. My own childish terms for the faeries who appeared to me when I was about four years old was "ladies in my eyes"—so called because they seemed to reside in my head, behind my eyes. It must also be kept in mind that the Fates were similarly female spiritual beings.

With this information we can also see a truly astounding point-to-point correspondence between British faerie beliefs and Tibetan teachings concerning dakinis. The word *dakini* (Tibetan: *khadro*) translated literally means "sky-goer." Tsultrim Allione describes the dakinis as "mystical female beings who may appear in dreams, visions, or human form." They are primarily energy-beings, "the wisdom-energy of the five colors, which are the subtle luminous forms of the five elements."

Dakinis, like faeries, are particularly associated with twilight; they frequently appear at twilight. They speak a mysterious non-rational "twilight language" (Sanskrit: *sandhyabhasa*) which can only be understood through the operation of another mode of knowing. Like faeries, they are "between-creatures," appearing and disappearing in the mysterious radiance of another world.

By comparing dakini to faerie we can discover one of the lost keys of the Faerie Tradition: every woman, every life situation can suddenly reveal itself as the energy-play of the dakini. Tsultrim Allione explains it thus:

> *The world is not as solid as we think it is, and the more we are open to the gaps, the more wisdom can shine through and the more the play of the dakini energy can be experienced.*

In the same way, any situation can reveal itself as the play of the powers of Faerie. Any woman can be a faerie. The old woman who initiated Anderson described herself as a faerie; because he had been able, briefly, to peer through the gaps in the ego's defenses, he saw her as just that. Dakinis do not teach in a linear, sequential left-brain manner. They transmit their wisdom directly through symbolic action and life experience. The dakini twilight language is essentially the same as the right-brain "starlight vision" described by Starhawk in *The Spiral Dance:*

> *The starlight vision…sees the universe as a dance of swirling energies…[It] does not postulate duration, a future or a past, a cause or an effect, but a patterned, timeless whole.*

Dakinis, again like faeries, represent the subtle flow of energies in natural phenomena. When this energy flow is, wittingly or unwittingly, disturbed, the dakini is also disturbed, and can even become hostile. In the same way, when a spring is dammed up, a stream diverted, or a wood cut down, the faeries presiding over such sites can become angered and annoyed. This is a leading theme in many European faerie tales.

Another vital correspondence between the dakini and faerie traditions is the matter of hidden treasures. In the twilight language, an entire text could be condensed into a single symbol and then hidden in various natural phenomena such as rocks, trees, or water. Yeshe Tsogyel, consort of Padmasambhava, took his teachings and hid them in "diamond rocks, in mysterious lakes and unchanging boxes." These places were protected by guardian spirits, who allowed them to be discovered only by people they deemed worthy. In just such a way, faerie treasure could only be discovered by a pure-hearted explorer; anyone else who overstepped the boundaries was tormented by the faerie hordes until he or she returned the stolen object, or was otherwise accursed. This also gives us a fascinating glimpse of the real nature of the faerie treasure-troves.

It should be noted that the dakini teachings are embedded in the Buddhist philosophy of the impermanence of all material objects and mental states. As we have seen, one meaning of the word faerie relates to the delusive and illusory nature of the worldly show. However, in the Buddhist scheme of things, material reality is only illusory insofar as one grasps at it (*sithich*, derived from *sith*, means "a sudden attempt to grasp"), and in this grasping attributes a fixed, immutable identity to what is, in essence, fluid and unbounded. This doctrine of the egolessness of all things is implicit in the paragraph by Starhawk quoted in the Prologue: if reality is "a field of energies that congeal, temporarily, into forms," then the forms have no real, independent existence.

How can these two world-views be so similar? One answer is that they both reflect the existence of real spiritual beings, energy-beings, normally hidden from our everyday vision. There is another answer. The dakini teachings derive ultimately from Orgyen, known as "the land of the dakinis," which existed in ancient times, northwest of India. It is possible that we have a memory here of a center of the worldwide matrifocal culture of the late Neolithic period, which flowered so magnificently at Çatal Hüyük, Malta, and in the Indus Valley. The faerie world-view derived from this same cultural matrix.

We can infer, then, that faeries are energy-beings of a particular type, "spirtual maidens of the forests and elements." However, this is not to deny the existence of male faeries. In the Tibetan tradition, the male equivalent of dakini is daka. The Fatuae had a male form also: Fatui. The female nature of the faeries is preponderant because the teachings come ultimately from a female-centered society.

It is now time to dispose of a few myths about the nature of faeries. The first is that they are always, and essentially, diminutive creatures. Certain orders of the faerie host do appear to psychics and sensitives as small beings, but even these can change size according to whim. Other orders, as we shall see, are human-sized or much taller.

This is an important point, because some ethnologists have sought to explain faerie beliefs as originating from the race memory of a smaller Lappish-like people, who may have been the Picts. Walter Evans Wentz, in his monumental work *The Fairy-*

Faith in Celtic Countries, disposes of such theories neatly. He points out that pygmy-like races still exist—in Southern Asia, Melanesia, New Guinea, and Central Africa—and they themselves have a faerie faith which includes the belief in smaller spiritual beings.

It is likely, observes Wentz, that sightings of diminutive spiritual creatures represent accurate reflections of existent entities, not folk memories of a race of dwarves.

The second myth is that faeries are the shrunken remnants of the Celtic gods and goddesses, who were virtually destroyed by the advent of Christianity. Again, this is a crucial point. We will be working later in the book with some of the forms of the Celtic Faerie Faith—but it should not be forgotten that the Faerie Way immeasurably predates the Celts.

We can see this by looking at the basic ground plan of the Faerie Way as it has been handed down through the Celtic tradition. In this tradition the Faerie race is called the Tuatha de Danaan, the people or tribes of the goddess Dana. In the *Leabhar na h-Uidhre,* written down in medieval times but preserving far earlier oral sources, we read that the Tuatha de Danaan were called "Siabhans," i.e., faeries. This alerts us to the fact that the Tuatha were always a spiritual race, inhabiting the energy dimensions. To look for them in the pages of history would be futile.

In the tale of the Battle of Moytura, written down initially in the sixteenth century but again deriving from far earlier oral sources, we read "The Tuatha De Danaan were in the northern islands of the world, studying occult lore and sorcery, druidic arts, witchcraft and magical skills, until they surpassed the sages of the pagan arts."

The term "northern islands" indicates the true home of the Tuatha, in the spiritual dimensions. The text continues, "They studied occult lore, secret knowledge, and diabolic arts in four cities: Falias, Gorias, Murias, and Finias."

What is being revealed here is a Mandala: Gorias in the East, Finias in the South, Murias in the West, and Falias in the North. However, there is also a mysterious fifth city, not mentioned in this text (See Chapter Nine). We saw above that dakinis are the wisdom-energy of the five colors; these five colors also represent the five elements and five directions. The five cities of the Tuatha de Danaan represent, therefore, a comprehensive glyph of Faerie wisdom-energy.

According to Fiona Macleod (who will be discussed later), the four cities are situated at the four points of the "green diamond that is the world." The fifth city, shaped like a heart, is situated centrally. The complete form has an ancient lineage and can be compared to the most ancient Neolithic images of the four lunar phases (see Figure 1).

Connected with this glyph, in both dakini and faerie traditions, are five wisdoms. We can see that the Tuatha de Danaan acquired their knowledge by connecting directly with these five points of the wisdom-energy of the universe. We will work with the five cities later, but for the moment it is enough to realize their ancient lineage and their connection to the energy realm.

The energy dimension is all around us at this moment. Our world, the green world of common experience, is being constantly created and recreated out of its swirling light, color, and sound. Other spiritual traditions speak of its existence. The great Sufi master and poet Muhyiddin Ibn Arabi describes inhabitants of the "Earth of True Reality" or the "Earth of Light":

> *In that Earth there are gardens, paradises, animals, minerals....Everything that is to be found on that Earth, absolutely everything, is alive and speaks, has a life analogous to that of every living being endowed with thought and speech. Endowed with thought and speech, the beings there correspond to what they are here below, with the difference that in that celestial earth, things are permanent, imperishable, unchangeable; their universe does not die.*

So, in the Earth of Light, in Faerieland, the animals talk. Even the stones talk! Furthermore, there are many species of animals there which we have never seen on our Earth. Whenever any one of us seeks to approach the Earth of Light, one of its natives immediately hurries toward us—"an ally of immeasurable benevolence."

We ourselves are, in fact, a part of the celestial earth, for our homologue (living semblance or image) exists there in a body of luminous fibers. These fibers have subtle, delicate extensions that reach to the borders of the green world. This "living double" is

Neolithic Images of the Moon

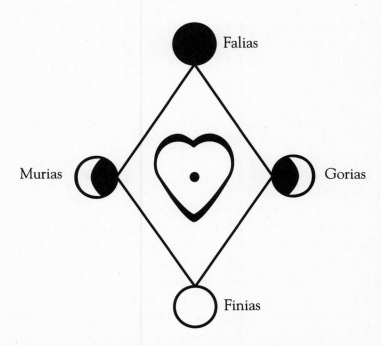

The Four Cities and the Phases of the Moon

FIGURE 1

the "Co-Walker" mentioned in the Faerie teachings. (Exercises will be given later to enable you to experience your Co-Walker's reality for yourself.)

Faerieland is a parallel dimension, coexisting with our own. We are intimately connected to it by the luminous fibers radiating from our light bodies. In many aspects, it is an energy counterpart of the physical Earth, with the light fibers acting as a means of transmission of energy between the two, like high-powered electric cables. But there are many animals and beings unique to Faerieland.

As I have said, we will learn to see the Faerie realm in detail later in the book. But just now, for a moment, close your eyes, and rest your mind in the space before thought. In that space, which is referred to in the teachings as a dimensionless point, and whose symbol is a palm tree, is the entrance to Faerieland. Before the mind breaks up the flow of experience into discrete observable quanta; before it pigeonholes every sense-datum into its vast filing system, there briefly arises the shining realm of Faerie.

Another derivation of Sidhe relates to the root meaning "peace." The Sidhe are "the People of Peace." We have seen something of the Neolithic source of the glyph of the five cities. It is probable that much of the Faerie symbology derives ultimately from the Neolithic period of prehistory (c. 10,000 B.C.– c. 5500 B.C.). This period is known to have been a predominantly peaceful one. Great cities were built at Mohenjo-Daro and Çatal Hüyük without any encircling walls to protect them. It is only with the invasions of the Kurgan warriors from the east beginning c. 4300–4200 B.C. that archaeologists begin to find carbonized areas indicating violent attack.

Within this peaceful Neolithic civilization, which had centers in Anatolia, India, and the area designated "Old Europe" by archaeologist Marija Gimbutas, we can find most of the major symbols of the Faerie Way, including the "tree of life," the long-eared dog or hound, the hart, and the hind—all of which we shall encounter in these pages. In addition, many thousands of figurines, relief images, and pottery designs of the Goddess have been recovered from this culture, indicating that it was predominantly matrifocal. The importance of the Goddess to the Faerie Way cannot be overstated, and seems to be a direct inheritance from the Neolithic past.

Marija Gimbutas, in her book *The Language of the Goddess*, describes the Neolithic world-view thus:

> *The Goddess in all her manifestations was the symbol of the unity of all life in Nature. Her power was in water and stone, in tomb and cave, in animals and birds, snakes and fish, hills, trees and flowers. Hence the holistic and mythopoeic perception of the sacredness and mystery of all there is on Earth.*

This could be an encapsulation of the Faerie Way as well. Almost certainly Faerie beliefs in both their Eastern and Western forms radiated from the Neolithic matrifocal culture. To look at the pottery and sculpture of this culture is to see the swirls, chevrons, and spirals of the energy realm underlying matter, and to recover a sense of the sacredness of everyday experience, both important concepts in Faerie beliefs.

Although this wonderful culture was destroyed by invading hordes, it has left a legacy for us of the late twentieth century—hidden in ancient designs, sacred stones, and fragments of old tales. If we look for this treasure, perhaps we will find that once again the People of Peace, The Shining Ones, are upon their ancient hills and about their ancient altars. We will truly practice the old ways.

CHAPTER TWO

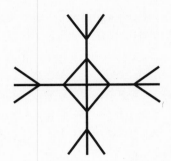

The UFO Connection

On a cold, dry day in January toward the end of the last century, a young man came face to face with one of the Gentry, or faeries, beneath the fog-shrouded heights of Ben Bulben in County Sligo. The faerie being was "dressed in blue with a headdress adorned with what seemed to be frills." He warned the young man that a girl of the faerie race had designs on him, and wished to spirit him away. He also requested that he not fire his gun, as the Gentry disliked the noise.

The young man later recounted his experience to the researcher Walter Evans Wentz. In response to Wentz's questioning he went on to give a description of the faeries which is unsurpassed in its accuracy, fullness, and richness of detail. The description can be condensed into fourteen salient points:

1. The Gentry or faeries are "a military aristocratic class, tall and noble-appearing."

2. "They are a distinct race between our race and that of spirits."

3. They are powerful enough to destroy half the human race but refrain from doing so out of ethical considerations.

4. They can strike human beings down with paralysis.

5. Their sight is much more sharp and penetrating than that of humans. It is almost as if they could "see through the earth."

6. They travel greatly throughout Europe, particularly favoring Spain, southern France, and the south of Europe.

7. They take a keen interest in human affairs, and always stand for justice and right.

8. "They take young and intelligent people who are interesting. They take the whole body and soul, transmuting the body to a body like their own."

9. They are ever-young.

10. Once humans taste food in faerie palaces, they cannot return to their own land.

11. They dislike salt, but eat fresh meat and drink pure water.

12. They marry and have children. They can, in certain circumstances, marry mortals.

13. They can appear in various forms. One appeared to Wentz's informant, seeming to be only four feet high. He said, "I am bigger than I appear to you now. We can make the old young, the big small, the small big."

14. "They have a silvery voice, quick and sweet."

Several of these points assume an interesting and somewhat disturbing new significance if we think of them in terms not of ancient myth, but of modern UFO research. This is not a new approach. Over twenty years ago, the French astrophysicist and computer scientist Jacques Vallee suggested a correlation between faerie myth and belief about faeries and modern UFO sightings in his classic book *Passport to Magonia*. Vallee's current view is that the two apparently separate phenomena derive from a common source: human interaction with beings from "other dimensions beyond spacetime." In *Dimensions: A Casebook of Alien Contact*, he writes:

I believe that the UFO phenomenon is one of the ways through which an alien form of intelligence of incredible complexity is communicating with us symbolically. There is no indication that it is extraterrestrial. Instead, there is mounting evidence that it has access to psychic processes we have not yet mastered or even researched.

As we have seen, the faeries are connected with just such an other dimension—the energy dimension or Earth of Light—and as we will see, they also teach by symbolic interaction. It seems that the phenomena of UFO and faerie encounters are intimately connected, if not actually the same.

Indeed, Vallee uses the classic work *The Secret Commonwealth of Elves, Fauns and Fairies*, written by the Reverend Robert Kirk in 1690 or 1691, almost as if it were an early treatment of the UFO enigma. We will study this work in some detail later. For the moment it is sufficient to observe that Kirk does illuminate the enigma to an astonishing degree. He speaks, as does the text quoted above, of humans abducted bodily into Faerieland. Even small details, such as his observation of the perpetually and steadily burning lights in the faeries "homes" (he had obviously never seen electric light), assume a new significance if placed in a UFO context.

Vallee explores the scientific possibility of interdimensional contact. He mentions the current belief among physicists involved in superstring research that the universe evolved from a ten-dimensional string that was unstable. Six dimensions have "curled up," leaving us the four-dimensional universe of our common experience. It may be helpful to think of the Earth of Light, or Faerieland, as one of these "curled up" dimensions. In 1926, the Swedish mathematician Oscar Klein suggested that the fifth dimension was "curled up" into a circle so small it could not be observed. It will be recalled that the entrance to the Earth of Light is just such a dimensionless point.

The system of symbolic communications which is the UFO phenomenon, functions at a global level, according to Vallee: "They [the UFO entities] are part of the environment, part of the control system for human evolution." Again, we could say exactly the same about the faeries. By acting as mirrors for us, the faerie people spur us on to evolutionary growth. They reveal to us both the horror of what we are and the glory of what we could be. The Earth of Light is deeply enfolded in rock and stream, sky and meadow, as the touchstone of cosmic process.

By far the most compelling evidence that the UFO and Faerie phenomena are essentially the same comes from the writer and abductee Whitley Strieber. Strieber believes that the "visitors" (as he calls them) have both a physical and a non-physical reality, with the non-physical side possibly being primary. Like Vallee, he observes that they teach by symbolic demonstration. They can also, he notes, enter the mind and, to a certain extent, control thought. Essentially, they are technicians of the soul and can even, by some unknown means, draw it out of the body. "We recycle souls," they told Strieber.

The parallels with the Faerie Way are astounding. Through his contact with the visitors, Strieber acquired the power of prophecy, foreseeing the terrible nuclear power plant accident at Chernobyl in 1986. As we shall see, prophecy is the particular province of the "forecasting invisible people" known as faeries. In one of his nocturnal encounters with the visitors he wears a white paper shift, a garment associated in a Welsh folk tale with the dance of the faeries.

Not only that, but Strieber visits places in dreams and visions which are obviously the Faerie cities of Falias and Gorias. He finds himself flying over a huge golden city with stadiums of light (Falias); or dancing in a maze path in an ancient desert "university" (Finias).

Strieber draws attention to the derivation of the names of many UFO entities from Gaelic originals. For example "Linn-Erri," who communicated with an amateur radio operator in 1961, derives from "Lionmhaireacht" (abundance). "Korendor" comes from "Cor Endor" (castle, circle, or mound of Endor). "Aura Rhanes," who appeared in 1952, derives her name from "Aerach Reann" ("heavenly body of air"). "Fir Kon" means "man of Conn," Conn being a seventh-century Irish king whose son was abducted by a faerie maiden in a flying crystal curragh. This last entity was a contact of the late George Adamski.

The Gaelic connection extends further. Leonard Keane has discovered that the star-language spoken by abductee Betty Andreasson Luca while under hypnosis was actually Gaelic. The translation of her words reads:

*The living descendants of the Northern peoples are groping
in universal darkness. Their [my] mother mourns. A dark
occasion forebodes when weakness in high places will revive
a high cost of living; an interval of mistakes in high places;
an interval fit for distressing events.*

Once again this is prophecy. The mother who mourns is
obviously Dana, Great Mother of the Northern peoples, whose
most popular form is Brigid. The emotional charge of this short
paragraph is intense. When Betty Andreasson Luca read the
translation, tears washed down her face. It is a message from the
Goddess to her wayward children in time. This message was
delivered through the medium of a supposed UFO abduction
experience.

All of this more than hints at the unity and identity of faerie
and UFO experiences. We have here the Goddess, we have
prophecy, and we have Gaelic, the language par excellence of the
faeries. We also have the basic philosophy of the Faerie Way.
Whitley Strieber sums up the impact of the visitors upon his consciousness thus:

*Throughout our history we have rejected the negative and
sought the positive. There is another way, I feel, that
involves balancing between the two. It is up to us to forge in
the deepest heart of mankind the place of reconciliation. We
must learn to walk the razor's edge between fear and
ecstasy—in other words, to begin finally to seek the full
flowering and potential of our humanity.*

As we shall see, the balancing of opposites is crucial to
progress in the Faerie Way.

It becomes apparent that UFO phenomena are merely the
current form of interaction with interdimensional entities previously labeled faeries, elves, lutins (shape-shifting sprites from
Normandy), nymphs, incubi, or succubi. Any UFO case can be
illuminated by this theory.

Take, for instance, the case of Maurice Masse. On July 1,
1965, Masse, a French farmer, surprised two dwarf-like entities in
his lavender field. They appeared to have landed in an egg-shaped
metallic craft no bigger than a car. One of the beings pointed a
small tube at Masse, and he was immediately rendered incapable

of movement. Even after the beings had departed, he was still unable to move. Alone in the field, and unable even to call for help, he became very frightened. Only after what seemed to be twenty minutes did he regain control of his movements and return home.

You will recall point four from above: the Gentry or faeries have the ability to strike humans down with paralysis; also point thirteen: they can appear any size they wish.

Another case can be similarly illumined. On October 12, 1963, between Monte Maiz and Isla Verda, Argentina, Eugenio Douglas saw three figures at least twelve feet tall appearing in the circular opening of a metallic craft about thirty-five feet high. They wore strange headdresses with antenna-like appendages. The beings directed a red ray of light at him, which followed him, turning the streetlights violet and green as he ran past.

These figures are highly reminiscent of the tall beings described by the Irish seer A.E., whose visions of faeries will be analyzed later in the book. These beings have rays of light emanating from their heads, which could well be described as antennae (see A.E.'s drawings, Plate 1).

If the UFO entities are the faeries in a new guise, we may have a set of powerful tools for interacting with them. Now that we know who they are, we can use the proven methods of the Faerie Way to control such an interaction.

For example, a UFO contact which has become forbidding or unwholesome could be ended through the use of the banishing ritual given in Chapter Six of this book. In fact, by using the techniques in this book, a richer and less one-sided relationship with the "visitors" might be cultivated. As Whitley Strieber says:

> If we choose to deepen our relationship with the visitors, I have no doubt that a much more fruitful interaction can be accomplished. This would represent a complete change in [our] relationship with this enigma. We would no longer be passive participants. Rather we would be to some small degree in coequal control of the relationship.

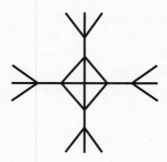

CHAPTER THREE

The Faerie Universe

In the beginning was the Goddess,
Dark and Light was She...

At the very beginning of the Faerie Way there stands a paradox—one perhaps difficult for the modern mind to comprehend. It is the paradox of darkness in light, of light in darkness—the complete and equal marriage of these two primal polarities.

The Western mind has been increasingly conditioned to think in terms of pairs of opposites, one "good," the other "bad." Hence our God-image has become split down the middle. Because God is only "good," all the negative effects which we observe in our life cannot be his work. They must be the work of an anti-God, ceaselessly undermining the work of his "good" counterpart. It has been said that the devil is the curse of those who have forgotten the Goddess.

This sort of dualistic thinking has no place in the world-view of Faerie. The Faerie Goddess contains and comprehends the full spectrum of life. Nothing exists outside Her orbit, and no malignant spirit strives to undo Her work. Whole and entire in Herself, She is all that is, was, or ever shall be.

As with light and darkness, so also with life and death. Starhawk, in her book *The Spiral Dance*, observes that "The nature of the Goddess is never single. Whenever She appears She embodies both poles of duality—life in death, death in life." She is both mother and destroyer—the beginning and the end, or consummation, of all that lives.

This concept is memorably and beautifully expressed by Fiona Macleod in *The Silence of Amor*. She speaks of Orchil:

> *The dim goddess who is under the brown earth, in a vast cavern, where she weaves at two looms. With one hand she weaves life upward through the grass; with the other she weaves death downward through the mould; and the sound of the weaving is Eternity, and the name of it in the green world is Time. And, through all, Orchil weaves the weft of Eternal Beauty, that passeth not, though her soul is Change.*

The implications of such a world-view are profound. To accept it—to accept the Dark/Light Goddess of life and death—is to recognize the holiness and sanctity of all life's cyclic processes. The Faerie initiate does not seek to escape from these cycles of becoming by entering some static Nirvana of eternal light. (After all, Orchil's shuttle weaves and unweaves the heaven-worlds of the Sidhe as well.) Rather, he or she aims to become fully alive within the system, navigating by the tides of life rather than attempting to dam or block them. Only by the acceptance of life's ceaseless changes can we discern the "weft of Eternal Beauty" that underlies them.

It follows from this that "bad" as well as "good" experience must be accepted from the hand of the Goddess. Obviously we do not have to seek out negative experiences purposely, but we must accept them when they come as inescapable teachers on life's way. The writer Robert Bly has noted that much New Age thinking is infected with what he calls "addiction to gold." This, he says, is a fixation with life's highs: the euphoric, expansive experiences (Maslow's "peak experiences") which we all have from time to time.

Bly's point is that we cannot have these experiences all the time. To do so would be pointless, growth-restricting, and ultimately boring—like a constant diet of cream cakes or caviar. Sometimes, for the sake of our own souls, we must take what he calls "the road of ashes, descent, and grief."

This is equivalent to the meeting with the Dark Goddess in the Faerie Tradition. And it is a vitally important spiritual key for us today, when New Age "addiction to gold" has led in some quarters to an actual denial of physical death.

I have said that the Goddess contains both light and darkness, initiates both birth and death. It must be clearly understood, however, that these polarities are not essentially separate and distinct in Her being. They interpenetrate and shade into each other.

For instance, Brigid, one of the primary aspects of the Faerie Goddess, presides over the hearth-fire, the center and focus of every home. She is thus "the mothering fire in the midst of the house," whose outstretched hands take our hands, sheltering and warming us in the depths of winter.

However, as the patron of smithery, She also holds the secrets of furnace and forge—the secrets of the red-hot vessel of transmutation, in which the sword (the sword of the spirit, we might say also) is heated and ruthlessly tempered. Brigid's hearth-fire can thus be seen as the entrance to the blazing and transformative world of the inner earth or underworld, the furnace/womb of the Earth Mother Herself. In Scandinavian/German mythology, this is the realm of the Goddess Hel. Our word "Hell" is derived from Her name. Yet Hel, as well as being Queen of the Underworld, rules as Faerie Queen of Summerland. We come full circle to the light again—the true meaning of Hel's name is "light," that light within the Earth that the Faerie initiate seeks to experience and mediate.

This perpetual circulation of light and dark within the Goddess must be considered when we come to work with the Dark Goddess later in this book. (See the pathworking in Chapter Nine.) In the Faerie Tradition the Dark One is known as "The Washer at the Ford," one of the guises of the Morrigan or "Great Queen." It is She who meets us at physical death, washing our soul clean and preparing it for rebirth.

That meeting is inescapable. But we may choose to meet Her during life, so that Her washing may remove outworn negative habits hindering our progress. She is the great deprogrammer, and it is sometimes necessary to unburden ourselves of the old emotional programs that cripple us.

Descriptions of the Washer are usually terrifying. Nikolai Tolstoy, in his novel *The Coming of the King*, describes an encounter with Her typically:

> *As the mist drew thicker between us, it seemed to me that beneath the surface of the water there lay heaped a cairn of mutilated heads and trunks and limbs, from whose open veins and pipes streamed gouts of blood which reddened all the river. It was but a glimpse I gained, and yet I fancy it was these the woman washed beneath the cloak she showed us.*
>
> *With this the Washer at the Ford departed from us, batwinged, lynx-taloned, and black as a scald crow; and we knew her to have come from the elf-mounds in the guise of a fair woman.*

The scald crow, or hooded crow, is the totem bird of the Morrigan, alerting us to the Washer's real identity. The horror of Her appearance—which is like the wrathful forms of the Tibetan bardo deities—should not blind us to Her essential nature, which is still "that divine compassion which exists beyond and is the final arbiter of the justice of the gods" (as A.E. puts it). She washes the clothes of slain heroes with deep pity for the human condition. And She will deal just as compassionately with us.

In the Faerie Tradition the dark aspects of life are recognized for what they are. There is no flinching. Yet they turn eternally in circuit with the light, and all is purified and renewed in the process. Death is necessary as a prelude to new life; darkness is needed so that the seed may germinate in the rich black soil. If all is eternally light, when may we dream?

For those who dare to confront Her, the Washer has great gifts to dispense, not least the gift of superhuman valor, which She gave to ancient heroes like Cuchulain. If we look at Her carefully and unflinchingly, we may see Her for what She is. The severed limbs She washes beneath the cloak are not the result of Her work, but of human folly and madness. She is merely cleaning up the mess, recycling the remnants with tenderness and pity.

The encounter with the Dark Goddess is thus an encounter with our own psychic waste material, our own "garbage." By facing Her we face our shadow-self, known in the Faerie Tradition as the Dark Fool, and named Dalua. Fiona Macleod describes the approach of this being:

I am the Fool, Dalua, Dalua!
When men hear me, their eyes
Darken: the shadow in the skies
Droops: and the keening woman cries
DALUA...DALUA...DALUA.

The "keening woman" is the Washer at the Ford, who often weeps or "keens" as She toils at Her grim task. In this She is closely related to the wailing banshee (from *bean-sidhe*, "woman-faerie"). As we approach the Washer, She in turn summons Dalua, the Dark Fool.

The connection between Dark Goddess and shadow-self is also found in Native American traditions. Arwyn Dreamwalker, a shaman of combined Celtic Irish and Native American descent, describes the Mayan mysteries thus:

In the Quetzalcoatl mysteries the Mayan calendar is based on [the] very complex fifty-two-year cycle of Venus: when it's the morning star, the evening star, and when it goes dark. During a period of darkness Quetzalcoatl descends into the Underworld, where he must face all the dark mirrors like in balancing the shields. As he rises, the Morning Star is the reconciliation of the dualities, it is the star of walking the beauty path.

Venus, of course, represents the Goddess, and the dark part of its cycle represents Her dark aspect. Like Quetzalcoatl, the Faerie initiate must journey into the Underworld (the realm of the faeries) to face the dark mirrors of the shadow-self. As we have seen in Chapter Two, the faerie peoples act as mirrors, reflecting both our light and our darkness back at us. They are living mirrors of the enigma of our own souls, in which darkness and light are intertwined. By meeting them, we meet ourselves—our own beauty and mystery—and rise transformed.

The Faerie Way is indeed a shamanic path, and its mysteries are not to be entered into lightly. Arwyn Dreamwalker describes the central shamanic experience of death and rebirth as "a melting down into death, crossing the threshold, giving away what must be given away, re-encoding and coming back out again into life."

As we have seen, the Washer at the Ford is the great re-encoder; and She is also the taker of anything that has outlived its usefulness in our lives. As we come to work with the Four Cities (and the fifth), we will see many parallels with the Native American "Balancing of the Shields." Balancing both Cities and Shields means bringing the forces of the cosmos into harmony within the individual psyche and, following from this, within the outer world also.

In fact, the Faerie Way and the way of initiation of the indigenous peoples of Turtle Island lead to similar, if not identical, core experiences. Only the imagery and symbolism used in each sets them apart. However, that imagery and symbolism is vitally important, as it was designed to interact with deeply encoded genetic keys. For peoples of European descent, the Faerie Way offers them their own shamanic path, their own beauty way to walk, that they may go to their Native American sisters and brothers not with empty hands, but with gifts of vision.

We have seen that darkness and light, life and death are interwoven in the Faerie Way. So also are the male and female. The Faerie Tradition, descending as it does from the predominantly matrifocal civilization of the megalith builders, stresses the primacy of the Goddess: Dana is known as the "Mother of the Irish Gods." This does not mean that the figure of the God is in any way ignored or devalued. It does mean, however, that what occultist William G. Gray calls "our feminine fundamental" is honored in this tradition.

Starhawk expresses this truth memorably in *The Spiral Dance* when she speaks of the Goddess falling in love with Her own reflection, "Miria, the Wonderful." The ecstasy of their love, however, sweeps Miria away, and she becomes progressively more masculine as her distance from the Goddess increases. Miria's first masculine guise is Dian-y-Glas—"the Blue God, the gentle, laughing God of love," equivalent to Angus Og in the Gaelic pantheon with which we will be working.

This profound myth indicates the primal unity of God and Goddess, male and female. The Great Mother is gynandrous, i.e., containing both polarities or genders within Her being. But the

God also contains the Goddess as his "feminine fundamental," and his journey around the Wheel of the Year is fueled by the desire to return to that blissful primordial unity. In the Faerie Tradition, we honor the Female as prime parent.

But we also honor the Male, as his deepest self is a reflection of the Goddess. This fusion and interpenetration of the sexes makes possible the adoption of far more fluid gender roles than those allowed by patriarchal religions.

We come now to another pair of polarities of special importance, whose divorce in our culture has led us to the brink of ecological catastrophe: matter and spirit. In the Faerie Way these are not seen as separate, exclusive modes of being, but as aspects of a stupendous Totality. Wherever we look in the Universe we cannot find one without the other.

This concept is well-illustrated by an example given by a seventh-century Buddhist teacher, Fa Ts'ang. Fa Ts'ang taught a variant of Buddhism, called Hua-Yen or Kegon, which drew on deep shamanic roots from Central Asia. These roots probably stretched back into the late Neolithic period, which we have seen was the formative period of the Faerie faith. Certainly, Hua-Yen has profound affinities with the world-view expressed by Kirk in his aforementioned analysis of faerie lore and beliefs, *The Secret Commonwealth of Elves, Fauns and Fairies* (see Chapters Two and Four).

Fa Ts'ang compared the universe to the statue of a golden lion. The gold from which the statue was made, he said, represented spirit or energy; the lion form of the statue represented matter. No matter how hard one tried, it would be impossible to separate the gold from the lion. They are inextricably fused in one entity. In just the same way the Universe is a seamless melding of spirit and matter.

Patriarchal religions have consistently tried to separate the inseparable, and create a "good" spiritual world in opposition to the "evil" realm of matter. The consequences of this meddling have been profound: it has led to our present attitude of domination of nature—"good" spirit disciplining "bad" matter—and our devaluation of the sacred Mother Earth.

For the Faerie initiate, every tree, every flower, every blade of grass is alive with its own indwelling spirit. Everywhere she or he looks there is "gold" and "lion." Moreover the follower of the

Faerie Way does not seek to command such beings, magical sword in one hand, spellbook in the other, like a medieval magician. Cooperation, not compulsion, is the watchword.

At this point in time it is vital that we realize the Earth is not expendable. We cannot leave it a scorched cinder while we journey through space in search of a more ideal realm. It contains all that we need and, more importantly, it is all we have. Our Earth Mother guards secrets we have only just begun to fathom.

This leads to an important aspect of the indissoluble unity of matter and spirit: the existence within the Earth, and within the larger universe, of many dimensions of being. This is also a feature of the ancient cosmology preserved in Hua-Yen Buddhism and the Faerie texts. Nothing moves or exists within the Universe that does not have smaller entities moving upon it, or larger ones encircling it. There are worlds within worlds ad infinitum, interpenetrating each other without obstruction.

This concept of the interfusion of planes is a vital key within the Faerie Tradition. It is radically different from the rigidly hierarchical model of the universe found in standard Western occultism, and has more in common with Aboriginal traditions of the Alcheringa or Dreaming. At this point we must realize that all of the realms we will learn to enter in this book—the Underworld of the sacred ancestors and the various planes and subplanes of the Sidhe—are separated for the sake of logical convenience only. In practice we will find them swirling together, interconnected in the eternal now with our own "green world" of common experience.

Every spring or stream carries to us the voices of our foremothers and forefathers from the Underworld; and in every breeze that blows we can hear the faint clash of the lances of the faerie host.

The world of the Sidhe or faeries is just one of these "Otherworlds" interpenetrating the space occupied by our home planet. But it is an important one, because it preserves the perfect pattern of our own world, being the first manifested world, the World of Immortal Youth. Our Earth Mother is weary of centuries of rape and despoliation, and sick with the poisons we have excreted upon Her body. Yet She may be refreshed at the fount of beauty that perpetually gushes in the Faerie realms and be healed of Her wounds. This is why it is vitally important that as many people as possible interact with the denizens of Faerieland, so the positive symbiotic relationship which once existed with these beings may be restored.

As noted earlier, the faeries exist in a mirroring relationship with us, and until we wake up to what is going on around us, they will bring us our worst nightmares, those dark aspects of ourselves and our world we dare not face. That is why I have stressed the initiations of confronting the Dark Mother and the shadow. However, if we persist in seeking to obtain these creatures' cooperation and trust, we will find the darkness radiant with fluorescent colors, pulsating and unfolding into the paradisal template of the first created world. And we will meet friends from whom we were parted before the worlds began.

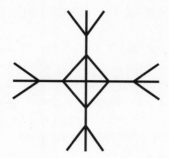

Four Great Seers

As we have seen, the roots of the Faerie Tradition seem to stretch into the immemorial past. The tradition has always had its great seers and teachers, many of whose names have been lost in the mists of time. Yet their teachings remain, encoded in the stone of ancient monuments and carvings, hidden in legends, concealed in old ballads, written on the wind.

Fortunately for the student, some seers and teachers have left their mark on the historical record as well. Brief biographies of four of these follow. All except the first (Thomas of Erceldoune, who still exists predominantly in the world of legend) have left a coherent body of work behind, from which we may learn. Yet all, without exception, are accessible in the timeless inner worlds as teachers for the students of today—and tomorrow.

Later exercises will aim at fostering a strong inner contact with one or more of the following seers, when your vision will open up to their teachings. In preparation for this experience, try to get the "feel" of the individual personalities as you read the biographical material and ask yourself which of them appeals to you most and why.

We begin at the intersection of legend and history.

Thomas of Erceldoune

Thomas of Erceldoune or Thomas Rhymer lived in thirteenth-century Scotland. He was probably born between 1210 and 1220, and may have survived until as late as 1307. Thomas was famous as a poet and prophet throughout England and Scotland. Robert Mannyng of Brunne, a contemporary of Thomas, celebrated him as the author of "an incomparable romance of the story of Sir Tristrem."

As a prophet, Thomas commanded respect and even awe. Something of the mantle of the ancient Celtic bard clung to his shoulders. An Aberdeenshire tradition gives us an unforgettable picture of his appearance before Fyvie Castle, whose gates had stood open "wall-wide" for seven years and a day, awaiting the arrival of "True Tammas." Suddenly he appeared, accompanied by a raging storm of wind and rain, which stripped the leaves from the surrounding trees and blew the castle gates shut with a loud crash. In ringing tones he announced the ruin of Fyvie. The storm continued to rage around him, but where the prophet himself stood there was not wind enough to move a blade of grass or a hair of his beard.

The accuracy of Thomas's prophesies elicited widespread admiration. When James VI ascended the English throne, Robert Birrell wrote in his diary that "the whole commons of Scotland that could read or had understanding were daily speaking and expounding on the prophecies of Thomas Rhymer, and other prophecies of ancient times." This was because Thomas had foretold the union of England and Scotland, in the ninth degree of Robert the Bruce's blood, three hundred years before the event!

The prophecies also received rapt attention during the Jacobite rising of 1745. The "Whole Prophecies" of Thomas Rhymer continued to be published as a chapbook until the beginning of the nineteenth century, when few farmhouses in Scotland were without a copy.

How did Thomas acquire such astonishing powers? A careful study of the "Ballad" and "Romance" of Thomas the Rhymer will provide an answer to this question. The "Ballad" was first committed to writing at the beginning of the nineteenth century, in two slightly differing versions. The editors of both versions believed that they derived from a genuinely ancient source. The "Romance," in contrast, was completed shortly after 1400 (i.e., about a hundred years after the Rhymer's death)—and there is an outside chance that its ultimate source was a work by Thomas himself.

Both poems are of such importance as repositories of Faerie lore that translations of them are provided in Appendix One. Both works suggest that the source of Thomas's uncanny powers lies in his catalytic encounter with the Queen of Elfland "down by the Eildon tree."

The "Ballad" tells the story thus: Thomas lies sleeping on a grassy bank beneath the Eildon tree—a hawthorn, long sacred to the powers of Faerie. Looking up, he beholds, a "lady gay" riding towards him over the fern-covered hillside. She is incomparably beautiful, wearing a skirt of "grass green silk," and mounted on a "milk-white steed" whose mane is plaited with silver bells. Perhaps it is the sound of these tiny bells, jingling as the horse moves, that has awakened him from his slumber. He springs up, doffing his hat and bowing low, and greets the stranger:

All hail, thou mighty Queen of Heaven!
For your like on Earth I never did see!

The lady immediately corrects him. She is not the queen of Heaven, but the "Queen of fair Elfland," and Thomas must go with her and serve her "through good and bad" for a period of seven years.

Thomas does not hesitate. He springs up behind her on the horse, and away they go, the silver bells ringing as they fly faster than the wind. The ordinary, everyday world of middle-Earth is left far behind and the sun and moon are eclipsed, as they wade through a great river of blood which reaches "to the knee." There is no sound in this darkness but the persistent "roaring of the sea."

For forty days and forty nights this state continues. Then suddenly, they are out into the light—not the light of sun or moon, but the soft radiance of the inner earth. They are in a beautiful garden, and before them stands an apple tree. Thomas offers to pick its fruit to give to the lady.

Again, however, she admonishes him. All the plagues of Hell, she explains, are contained within the fruit of this country. However, recognizing his hunger (unsurprising after forty days and nights of solid riding!), the lady produces from her lap a loaf of bread and a bottle of claret wine. These they share.

After this repast the lady invites Thomas to rest with his head on her knee. As he takes his ease she shows him three marvels. These are the three roads: the broad road of wickedness, which some mistake for the road to Heaven; the narrow road of righteousness, overgrown with thorns and briars; and the "bonny" road to fair Elfland, winding circuitously about the hillside ahead.

It is to Elfland that Thomas and the lady must go this very night. But before they set off she warns him that whatever marvels he might chance to see in that country, he must hold his tongue. For if he speaks one word he will never get back to his own world.

The "Ballad" does not allow us any glimpses into Elfland. In the final verse we see Thomas attired in a green coat of "even" cloth and green velvet shoes—gifts from the Queen of Elfland in token of his service. He is now, presumably, ready to return to middle-Earth to begin his prodigious career as poet and prophet. He brings with him all the powers of Faerie, including a last and most precious gift from the Queen: the tongue that cannot lie.

There is no doubt that the "Ballad" preserves a potent sequence of initiatory images. However, although the "Ballad" preserves the order of the sequence, several important keys to its understanding seem to be missing. These are to be found in the "Romance" which may indeed preserve the personal reminiscence of the Rhymer himself (the frequent lapses into the first person indicate as much).

The "Romance" differs from the "Ballad" in several significant details, the first of which involves the description of the lady. "Seven hounds by her they ran," records the author of the

"Romance." This takes us back to the ancient roots of Goddess worship in Neolithic Europe. Anne Baring and Jules Cashford observe in their book *The Myth of the Goddess* that "the culture of Old Europe reveals the very ancient origin of the link between dog, dark moon, black night and goddess." One of the variants of the "Ballad" contains the line, "It was mirky night and there was no starlight."

The link between the dog or hound, the Goddess and the powers of Faerie is an important key. A dog painted on a pear-shaped vase dating from about 3500 B.C., and found in Moldavia, closely resembles the Faerie long-eared hound. And on vases from Cucuteri (eastern Romania and western Ukraine) from about the mid-fourth millennium B.C., dogs guard the Tree of Life, primal symbol of the Goddess Herself (See Figure 2). As we have seen, the Queen of Elfland guides Thomas to this Tree, the sacred apple tree of madness and poetic inspiration.

The elfin hounds reappear at intervals throughout the "Romance," lapping at the blood running from haunches of venison at the Faerie Castle, and straining at their leashes during the long final meeting between Thomas and the queen.

We seem to have here a strong indication that Thomas is being initiated into the mysteries of the Dark Goddess of death, rebirth, and transformation.

Dogs, of course, traditionally guard the entrance to the realm of the dead. This is born out by the queen's reference to her husband:

> My lord is so fierce and terrible
> That is king of this country.

Together with the various references to Hell, this seems to indicate that the king is a Plutonian figure, which would equate the lady with Persephone, Queen of the Underworld.

Persephone, however, is by the derivation of Her name, "she who shines in the dark." And Thomas's lady, the Queen of Elfland, also has her radiant, light aspect. When he first sees her, the text of the "Romance" records:

> As does the sun on a summer's day,
> That lady herself she shone.

Dog, circa 3500 B.C. *(Soviet Moldavia)*

Dogs Guarding the Tree of Life,
mid-fourth millennium B.C. *(Western Ukraine)*

Dogs and the Tree of Life,
mid-fourth millennium B.C. *(Western Ukraine)*

FIGURE 2

So his initiation is not into the powers of darkness alone, but into that light/dark polarity which we saw in Chapter Three as characteristic of the Goddess of the Faerie Way.

The second major difference between "Ballad" and "Romance" continues this theme. In the "Romance," Thomas actually has intercourse with the queen. Indeed he is such an ardent lover that she has to remonstrate with him:

> *You make merry with me all the live-long day,*
> *I pray you, Thomas, let me be!*

However, after their lovemaking a terrible change comes over her:

> *Her hair it hung all over her head,*
> *Her eyes seemed out, that before were gray,*
> *And all her rich clothing was away*
> *That he had seen before, instead;*
> *Her one leg black, the other gray,*
> *And all her body dull like lead.*

She has, in fact, turned from light to dark. This is the exact inverse—a sort of Underworld reflection or refraction—of the ancient myth of the Goddess of Sovereignty. One Irish version of this myth concerns Niall Noighiallach, who together with his four brothers finds himself lost in the wilderness. Each in turn goes off to look for water, and comes upon a well guarded by a hideous crone, who will give water only in return for a kiss. Three of the brothers refuse her demand. Fiachra grants her a grudging peck on the cheek, but Niall not only kisses her but agrees to lie with her as well. The result of his action is miraculous. The aged hag becomes a beautiful young girl, shining more radiantly than the sun. She reveals herself to be the Sovereignty of Ireland, and prophesies that Niall and his descendants will hold unbroken rule—except for two kings from the lineage of Fiachra in token of his grudging kiss.

The parallels with our tale are striking: Thomas's lady shines like the sun, but can also appear as a withered hag. In both cases the catalyst for the change is sexual. Like Niall, Thomas does not reject the lady in her ruined and ravaged state. Consequently, she is soon returned to her former beauty:

She became again as fair and good,
And also as rich on her palfrey…

A true initiate of the Faerie Way, he accepts both darkness
and light, the totality of existence as it is. Anne Baring and Jules
Cashford, speaking of the Goddess in the Grail legends, have this
to say: "Disguised as a hideous hag, she guides them [the knights]
to embrace their own darkness and transform it through love."

Thomas has embraced his own darkness without flinching,
and thus attained union with the Goddess of the Sacred Land.
The green coat and shoes awarded him by the queen are symbolic
tokens of this union. Now the Land itself may speak and prophesy
through his lips.

This theme of union with the Land is reiterated in four mysterious lines which occur only in the "Romance." They are
uttered by the lady immediately before her farewell at the end of
the first fit of the poem:

Far out in yon Mountain gray
Thomas, my falcon builds a nest,
A falcon is a heron's prey,
Therefore in no place may he rest.

As they stand these lines make no sense. Herons do not prey
on falcons! However, we find the theme of falcon and heron elsewhere in medieval literature. A ballad from oral tradition known
as the "Corpus Christi Carol" begins:

Lullay, Lullay, Lullay, Lullay,
The Falcon hath taken my make (mate) away
The heron flew east and the heron flew west,
She flew over a fair forest.

Moreover, in this same ballad we find other symbolic keys
familiar to us from the Thomas literature: (apple tree) orchard,
thorn tree, and hounds licking up blood. Obviously there is a
deep inner connection between "Carol," "Ballad," and
"Romance." One image presented in the "Corpus Christi Carol"
is particularly important: a sleeping knight upon a bed, whose
"wounds do bleed with main and might."

As in the Grail legends, this figure represents the wounded
land. We note that the orchard which surrounds the hall in
which he sleeps is "brown" or faded and withered.

So the apparently trivial detail of the falcon and heron alerts us to the fact that Thomas has been united with a "wounded" Land: a Scotland menaced by the bloody depredations of the English invasions, like the falcon, can take no rest. Henceforth, his prophetic role must take on a political character. It need not surprise us that the historical Thomas was probably a nationalist agent, and certainly closely associated with William Wallace.

It will be seen that Thomas's initiation breaks down naturally into three stages, each flowing into the next:

1. Contact (sexual or otherwise) with the Dark/Light Goddess.
2. Union with the land.
3. Recognition of the wounded nature of the land.

(Careful meditation on each of these stages—and their implications—is recommended before you attempt to pathwork the "Ballad" sequence.)

Thomas, therefore, returned to Earth after his seven years service in Faerie Land. We have already seen something of the awesome powers he acquired during his sojourn. But at the end of his long life the powers of Faerie claimed him again. The legend tells it thus: while Thomas was feasting with his friends in the tower of Erceldoune, a person came hurrying in to tell the assembled company of an astonishing marvel—a hart and hind had left the surrounding forest, and were slowly processing up the street of the village. Thomas said not a word. He recognized the sign that the Queen of Elfland had given him all those years ago. He arose on the instant, ignoring his guests, and followed the animals into the forest, never to return. According to popular belief he still "drees his weird" in Faerie Land, beneath the beautiful and legend-haunted Eildon Hills. One day, it is said, he will visit Earth again. The Eildon Tree, from beneath which he delivered many of his prophecies, no longer stands, but its site is marked with a stone.

One very interesting question remains: was Thomas involved with any organized form of the Faerie or Witch cult? There is some evidence that he may have been. The trial of Andro Man for witchcraft took place in Aberdeen in 1598. According to Andro's testimony, he was assured in his boyhood by the Queen of Elfin "that you should know all things, and should help and cure all sort of sickness, except [those] stone dead, and that you should be well-blessed, but must beg your bread as Thomas Rhymer did."

Andro was also charged that:

You affirm that the Queen of Elfin has a grip of all the craft [i.e., teaches all magic], but Christsondy [the devil] is the good man, and has all power under God, and that you know sundry dead men in their company, and that the King that died at Flodden and Thomas Rhymer are there.

Andro's testimony opens up some intriguing possibilities. Apparently Thomas was still accessible as a source of knowledge either on the inner planes or otherwise, three hundred years after his death or disappearance. There is also the possibility that "Queen of Elfin" was an honorific title applied to the high priestess of a coven or other group. This latter, of course, would not preclude her also being, at the same time, an innerworld entity.

I have dealt with Thomas at some length because he is such an important teacher of the Faerie Way. It is necessary to stress that he is as accessible now as he was to Andro Man in 1598. Indeed, there are those who would say that the Thomas Erskine cited as a "secret chief" by Dion Fortune and her circle was really another Thomas—Thomas of Erceldoune. If this is true, it would certainly explain the increasing Faerie contacts of that circle during the 1930s.

If you are seriously interested in the Faerie Way you will certainly meet him yourself at some point. Following is my own account of my first encounter with Thomas the Rhymer.

In 1988 I was a member of a magical group working a broadly Qabalistic system. I had no knowledge whatsoever of Thomas the Rhymer, beyond once having heard the folk rock version of the "Ballad" by the English band Steeleye Span. Our group meetings were usually decorous and dignified affairs, with a little discussion after pathworking or ritual. Thomas changed all that. One evening he exploded (I can think of no better word) into my inner vision. He was dressed as a medieval minstrel, and cut such comic and amazing capers that I had to burst out laughing—much to the rest of the group's discomfiture. Along with this eruption of color and (apparent) madness I heard three words: Thomas the Rhymer.

From that moment Thomas took over the helm of the group. He steered us deep into the waters of Celtic and Faerie myth, and (later) into Native American symbolism and lore. At the time the latter departure seemed like a detour, but I now realize that he was guiding us toward the recovery of several vital keys missing from our own tradition. Some of these keys are in this book.

Since then he has appeared to me many times, and in many forms. As a white-bearded ancient he presides at the semicircular altar of the cave of the ancestors—and is a vital and protective guide for all ancestral contact. My advice for anyone beginning to tread the Faerie Path is this: seek Thomas first. But remember, if you are sincere, he is equally capable of seeking you out.

Moving forward in time four hundred years, yet still remaining in Scotland, we come to our next great seer—and an intriguing historical mystery.

Robert Kirk

On the night of May 14, 1692, the body of the Reverend Robert Kirk, well-loved and respected minister of Aberfoyle in Perthshire, was found on the Faerie Knowe (hill) near his manse. He must have taken ill very suddenly while on a brief evening walk, as the body was clad only in a nightshirt.

Rumors immediately began to circulate that the Reverend Kirk had not in fact died, but had instead been abducted physically into Faerieland. The body found on the Knowe, it was said, was a mere "stock"—a simulacrum left by the faeries; the real Kirk was elsewhere.

These rumors acquired some substance when, shortly after the incident, Kirk appeared to his cousin, Grahame of Duchray. The minister confirmed to Grahame that he was still alive, but a prisoner in Faerieland. He could be freed, he said, only if Grahame followed his explicit instructions. The cousin must be present at the baptism of Kirk's posthumous child. Kirk would also appear at the baptism in spectral form, whereupon Grahame should throw a dirk over his ghost. The spell would then be broken.

At the christening, everything transpired as Kirk had foretold. The specter duly appeared, but Grahame, rooted to the spot in terror, was unable to throw the knife. So the Reverend Robert

Kirk remained a captive in the subterranean realm below the Faerie Knowe.

This belief persisted in Aberfoyle for many years. Much later, during the Second World War, an officer's wife rented Kirk's Manse. She was expecting a child, and was told by a local resident that if the christening was held there, and during it a dirk was stuck into Kirk's chair, he would be freed from his long captivity. For whatever reason (perhaps the lady was understandably skeptical) this was not tried. According to local belief, Kirk remains under the hill, and his tomb in the old churchyard of Aberfoyle contains nothing but stones.

Local tradition also unanimously records the reason for Kirk's abduction by the faeries: he had written too unguardedly of their hidden ways. Concerned lest he let slip any more faerie secrets, they had taken him as their own.

The historical Robert Kirk (1644–1692) was a deeply devout country minister who devoted himself to the translation of the psalms, the Bible, and the catechism into Gaelic. In this venture he was an assistant of Robert Boyle, the scientist known as "the father of modern chemistry." Yet he is chiefly remembered today for one extraordinary book, *The Secret Commonwealth of Elves, Fauns and Fairies* (written in 1690 or 1691, shortly before his "death"). We have already seen (in Chapter Two) something of the importance of this work. Now we need to tease out the further secrets it contains—secrets essential to the reconstruction and popular presentation of the ancient Faerie Way. Kirk himself was a seventh son and hence probably a seer. So at least some of these secrets may be the fruit of his personal experience.

The first point to be made is that Kirk, throughout *The Secret Commonwealth*, insists on the actual, literal reality of the faerie beings (or *siths*—the Scottish version of the Irish word Sidhe—as he calls them). They are a real people, with their own rulers and laws, their own houses, weapons, and books. Even though their bodies are subtler than our own, being of a "light, changeable" nature "like those called Astral, somewhat of the nature of a condensed cloud, and best seen at twilight," they can still produce real effects in our world.

This is a tradition nearer to the world-view of Native American shamanism and sorcery than to popular Western conceptions of faeries, elves, and the like. Kirk's "siths" more closely resemble Don Juan's formidable "allies" (as recorded in Carlos Castaneda's books) than they do J. M. Barrie's "Tinkerbell" from *Peter Pan*.

Indeed, Kirk relates a story which might have come straight from the pages of Castaneda: he has heard report, he says, of a man who was seen regularly disappearing from a particular place and reappearing, at the distance of a bow-shot, about one hour later. In the intervening time he fought furiously with his faerie "allies," sometimes wrestling with them, and on one particular occasion cutting a *sith* in two with an iron knife, to avoid the onset of the Second Sight.

Arwyn Dreamwalker, herself of Celtic Irish and Native American lineage, and a practicing shaman, expresses this actual reality of allies and Otherworlds forcefully in an interview:

> *The internal logic of what Castaneda writes about is totally real. I've done many of those things myself and seen other medicine people do them. People indeed walk up walls, walk through the gateways; those things are not fiction for native peoples.*

Hence Kirk's literal translation into the Otherworld, still believed by the people of Aberfoyle to this day; and hence also the very real powers of the Faerie initiate.

Such a connection with worldwide shamanistic techniques need not surprise us. As we have seen, the Faerie Way began in the remote past (at the very earliest the late Neolithic) when such methods were widespread.

Secondly, Kirk states as firmly that the *siths* or faeries exist in a mutually beneficial relationship with humanity; and that this relationship is the basis of the phenomenon known as Second Sight. The person with the Second Sight can foresee, predict future events. This occurs because he or she can perceive "the operations of these forecasting invisible people" (i.e., the faeries). Kirk adds that it is necessary to have the Second Sight in order to see the faeries in the first place.

He then proceeds to give two techniques for acquiring the "Sight." The first of these bestows full "seership" (i.e. permanent Second Sight), the second but grants a temporary glimpse.

The point of issue here is that Second Sight (what we would call psychic or inner vision) is a prerequisite of the Faerie Way. It is intimately connected to the prophetic vocation that we saw Thomas of Erceldoune assuming as a result of faerie contact. Kirk notes that those who have the "Sight" do not disclose things immediately when asked, like a fortune teller, but in "fits and raptures" like a prophet. Both Second Sight and prophecy are intimately connected to the land itself, and to the sacred ancestors.

Kirk connects the faeries to the land in several passages of *The Secret Commonwealth*. For instance, he suggests that they are divided into different tribes, depending upon the country under which they live, their clothing and speech mirroring that of the surface inhabitants. And in a particularly interesting section he links them with the Faerie Hills, in which the souls of the ancestors dwell. He even implies that the "Mount" dedicated beside every ancient churchyard to receive the souls of the dead eventually becomes just such a Faerie Hill.

Perhaps Kirk's most important contribution in *The Secret Commonwealth* is his preservation of the holistic philosophy of our remote ancestors, including the basic tenets of the Faerie Way:

> *For it is one of their Tenets that nothing perishes, but, as the Sun and Year, everything goes in a Circle, Lesser or Greater, and is renewed, and refreshed in its revolutions. As it is another that Every Body in the Creation moves, which is a sort of life, and that nothing moves but what has another Animal moving on it, and so on, to the utmost minute corpuscle that is capable to be a receptacle of life.*

These are staggeringly modern-sounding concepts, uniting the micro- and macro-levels of the universe in one holistic model. They also harmonize with modern discoveries in quantum physics which have revealed to us a universe interconnected in every particular. There are parallel passages in Eastern scriptures, for example, the Avatasamka Sutra, which speaks of one hair containing innumerable Buddha-worlds. But there is certainly nothing quite like it in the Western Esoteric Tradition!

Kirk also says that, according to the Faerie philosophy, "every Element and different state of being has [in it] Animals resembling those of another Element."

Again, the only parallel is with the Avatasamka Sutra, which describes the universe as a vast web of jewels (the Jewel

Net of Indra) with each individual jewel reflecting all the others. These similarities can be explained by the hypothesis that both the Buddhist Sutra and the Faerie philosophy outlined by Kirk draw on a common and very ancient cosmological model.

We note that the Circle or Wheel referred to above is both the Wheel of the Year, and the Wheel of Death and Rebirth. And it is in constant motion. According to Kirk, so are the Faeries, who "remove to other lodgings at the beginning of each Quarter of the year." The ceaseless passage of the faeries around the Wheel of Life is thus directly related to the passage of the seasons themselves, and to the life of the land. It is also related to the Four Cities of the *siths*, Sidhe, or Tuatha de Danaan (see Chapters One and Seven), and is the reason that the Fifth, central City is of such importance, being at the point of rest, repose, and balance.

In addition, Kirk mentions two important Faerie traditions which will be part of our program of practical work. The first is that of the "Leannain Sith" or Faerie Lovers. We have already seen the blessings attendant on Thomas's dalliance with such a one. There is no doubt that meeting one's Faerie Lover can be a catalytic and transformative experience for some, but it is not an exercise for everyone (details of this experience will be found in Chapter Eight). The second tradition concerns the *coimimeadh* or Co-Walker, the double of the Faerie initiate. The Co-Walker is, in fact, a special form of faerie ally. This exercise is more universally applicable (again, details may be found in Chapter Eight).

There is, apparently, one major omission in *The Secret Commonwealth*: at no point does Kirk mention the Goddess of the Faerie Way. As she played such an important part in the story of Thomas of Erceldoune, we may think this curious.

However, as R. J. Stewart has suggested, the Goddess is present in a hidden or veiled form within the pages of the book. Kirk mentions that the faeries' houses are lit by perpetual lamps and fires "often seen (burning) without fuel to sustain them." He also observes that the seers, or people of Second Sight, are surrounded by a beam of light which enables them to see both the faeries and forthcoming events. The faeries are also said to convey the power of healing to those who interact with them.

All these aspects point to a connection with Brigid, the great Celtic Goddess of fire and fertility. Brigid also had a perpetual fire, tended by nineteen maidens at Kildare in Ireland. She was associated with spiritual light, conveying illumination and understanding, and with the power of healing. Her cult was widespread throughout the Highlands and Islands of Scotland when Kirk was writing.

It must be remembered that even great initiates are not totally free from the cultural biases and assumptions of their day. Within the patriarchal framework of his time, Kirk said as much as he could.

And so perhaps we may leave the Reverend Kirk now, beneath the Faerie Knowe at Aberfoyle. Like Thomas he still "drees his weird" in Faerieland. However, the same proviso applies: He may also be contacted by the sincere student of the Faerie Way, and is a potent source of inner teaching. He is a particularly apt teacher for those working on the pagan/Christian interface, and also for those who are interested in the intricacies of the Faerie cosmology.

One final point may be made, touching upon the existence of a hidden order, or secret society, teaching the Faerie Way in Kirk's time. An intriguing hint of such a possibility occurs in a letter of 1699 from George, third Lord Reay of Durness in Sutherland, to Samuel Pepys, the famous diarist. Pepys, in his capacity as Secretary to the Admiralty, was interested in the Second Sight—primarily for its possibilities in the field of espionage. Lord Reay includes with his own a letter on this subject from Lord Tarbat, which Kirk also quotes in full in *The Secret Commonwealth*.

However, it is Reay's letter which is of interest here. He writes of a people in Scotland, surnamed "Mansone," who "have the Second Sight naturally, both males and females." On questioning one of these Mansones, Reay was offered an experience of the Sight, by a method closely resembling the one described by Kirk. However, Reay's Mansone said that he could not free the inquirer from seeing visions afterward, so the good Lord wisely declined the offer. This may be compared with the testimony of Andro Man in 1598, one hundred years earlier, which, as we have seen in our section on Thomas of Erceldoune, seemed to hint at some form of organized cult. Could these "Mansones" be descendants of Andro Man, heir to the wisdom of the Rhymer and the Queen of Elfland?

Our search for the great seers of the Faerie Tradition takes us forward again in time, and across the sea to Ireland.

A.E.

George William Russell (whose pen name was A.E.) was born in Lurgan, County Armagh, on April 10, 1867. His family soon moved south to Dublin, where the young A.E. attended Rathmines School and the Metropolitan School of Art. It was at the art school that he first encountered the poet William Butler Yeats. A friendship developed between the two men—who were both, in their different ways, pursuing the springs of inner vision—and despite occasional periods of strain, lasted their whole lives.

A.E. was a truly extraordinary man. Not only was he a poet, painter, essayist, journalist, and editor; he was also a perceptive economist with a special understanding of the problems of rural agriculture. During Franklin D. Roosevelt's first term of office, then-Secretary of Agriculture Henry Wallace invited A.E. to visit the United States and lecture on rural reorganization. Both the *London Times* and the *Dublin Times* regularly gave him editorial space to comment on current issues.

He was (like Thomas and Kirk before him) an eminently practical man, fully competent to engage with the day-to-day world on its own terms. But he was also a deeply intuitive seer and mystic who had lifelong communication with faerie beings. Yeats called him "a visionary who may find room beside Swedenborg and Blake."

Paul Brunton (author of *The Wisdom of the Overself* and other seminal books on Indian yoga) was taken under the elderly A.E.'s wing when he was just setting out on his own spiritual quest. A.E. gave the young Brunton some memorable advice: "Why go off to the East for light?" It should be just as possible, he said, to find union with the World Soul in the West—even in a city like Dublin!

Nevertheless, A.E. intuitively recognized and blessed Brunton's mission to bring the essence of the Eastern teachings to the West. And Brunton has left a glowing tribute to his friend and mentor. "A true Olympian" he says of A.E. in his Notebooks: "[M]y beloved friend... clairvoyant, seer and, when I met him, more of a sage."

So what did this practical, well-loved man see in the realms of Faerie? A.E. has left an astonishingly detailed acount of his visions, both in his beautiful prose writings and his numerous faerie paintings. Merely reading his descriptions, or seeing the images he so lovingly portrayed on canvas, can boost one's own powers of inner perception—an effect recognized both by Paul Brunton and Nevill Drury, the writer on occultism.

A.E. makes an initial distinction between "pictures seen in the memory of nature and visions of actual beings now existing in the inner world." The faerie visions are of the latter type. Moreover, by "inner world" he means the Celtic Otherworld, "though there are many Otherworlds." This realm, the Tir-na-nog of the ancient Irish, is the abode of the races of the Sidhe. It may be described as "a radiant archetype of this world."

We have here as firm an insistence on the actual reality of the *siths*, Sidhe or faeries in their own world as that expressed by Kirk in his *Secret Commonwealth*. They are real beings, not mere echoes or reflections of historical events.

A.E. classifies the Sidhe into two great races: the Shining Beings and the Opalescent Beings.

The Shining Beings are "lower in the hierarchy" than the Opalescent Beings, their lower order corresponding to the nature elementals. They are hive-beings with no individualized life, says A.E.: "thus if one of them raises his hands all raise their hands, and if one drinks from a fire-fountain all do." These Shining Beings are nourished by "something akin to electrical fluids." They are about our own height, or perhaps a little taller.

The Opalescent Beings, in contrast, seem "to hold the positions of great chiefs and princes among the tribes of Dana" (i.e., the Tuatha de Danaan). They are seen less frequently than the Shining Beings, and draw their nourishment directly from the Soul of the World. They possess a greater individuality, but also a greater spiritual unity than those of the Shining Tribes. They are about fourteen feet in stature.

Both classes of beings exist in male and female forms, and "forms which (do) not suggest sex at all." And both have only a relative immortality, being immensely longer-lived than men and women, but having eventually to die and pass into new bodies, as we do.

As for reproduction, the higher orders of the Sidhe seem capable of "breathing forth beings out of themselves." A.E. suggests that some of the Opalescent Beings act as "motherships" for elemental entities, which they send out and receive back into themselves again.

The Opalescent Beings are denizens of the heaven world, while the Shining Beings belong to the mid world. Our own earth world constitutes the third and lowest level of existence in this scheme (see diagram, Figure 3).

Obviously, these tall, beautiful beings bear little resemblance to the widespread concept of faeries as diminutive and charming sprites. But then, as we have seen, the popular "cute" image of the faerie has no basis in the original tradition. A.E. cites an old schoolmaster in the West of Ireland who referred to the Sidhe as "tall, beautiful people" and used some Gaelic words meaning that they shone with every color of the rainbow.

How does one see these beings? A.E. notes that it is easier to see them after being away from towns or cities for a few days. There are also places on Earth where the veil separating the

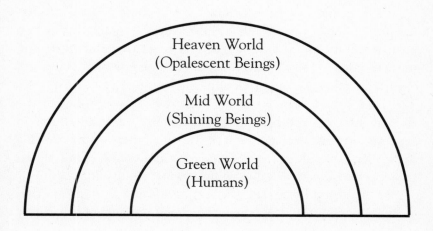

A.E.'s Schema of the Three Worlds

FIGURE 3

dimensions is thin—for example, the entire west coast of Ireland from Donegal to Cork, which, he observes, "seems charged with a magical power." Visions of the Sidhe come more easily to those who sojourn in such wild and romantic spots. Ancient sites also seem to draw them. A.E. gives the examples of New Grange and Dowth, but there are ancient monuments and ritual areas world-wide which can act as windows to the world of the Sidhe. This is because, as A.E. says, such sites "are naturally charged with psychical forces."

What follows is one of A.E.'s vivid descriptions of the Opalescent Beings. As you read it, relax and allow yourself to see the image with your inner eye.

> There was at first a dazzle of light, and then I saw that this came from the heart of a tall figure with a body apparently shaped out of half-transparent or opalescent air, and throughout the body ran a radiant electrical fire, to which the heart seemed the center. Around the head of this being and through its waving luminous hair, which was blown all about the body like living strands of gold, there appeared flaming wing-like auras. From the being itself light seemed to stream outward in every direction; and the effect left on me after the vision was one of extraordinary lightness, joyousness, or ecstasy.

(Note the similarity to Kirk's *siths*, whose "Astral" bodies resembled condensed clouds.) A.E.'s works—especially the two prose meditations "The Candle of Vision" (1918) and "Song and its Fountains" (1932)—are filled with such passages. They are essential reading for any student of the Faerie Way.

A.E. found that out of all the tribes and subtribes of the Sidhe, only the water-beings produced any negative effects in him. He dreaded the approach of these members of the Shining Tribes because it always heralded "a great drowsiness of mind" and in some cases "...an actual drawing away of vitality."

This antipathy did not prevent him from recording another extraordinary vision, this time of an elemental king of the watery realm:

> In the world under the waters—under a lake in the West of Ireland in this case—I saw a blue-and-orange-colored King

seated on a throne; and there seemed to be some fountain of mystical fire rising from under his throne, and he breathed this fire into himself as though it were his life. As I looked I saw groups of pale beings, almost gray in color, coming down one side of the throne by the fire-fountain. They placed their head and lips near the heart of the elemental King, and then, as they touched him, they shot upwards, plumed and radiant, and passed on the other side, as though they had received a new life from this chief of their world.

Elsewhere he describes wood beings "of a shining silvery color with a tinge of blue or pale violet, and with dark purple-colored hair."

The graphic nature of these descriptions flows no doubt from the skills of visual perception A.E. had developed in his painting. His faerie paintings are equally powerful. Several are reproduced here, as a stimulus to your own powers of inner vision (see Color Plates).

A.E.'s great contribution to the Faerie Tradition was his restatement of its central tenets in terms that had a strong appeal to the artists, thinkers and poets of his day. He was able, with his manifold skills, to reveal the real experience underlying what had hitherto been regarded as quaint folklore.

One part of this restatement was the restoration of the Goddess to a major place in the spiritual and theosophical thought of the time. A.E. wrote eloquently and often of Dana, "the Great Mother and Spirit of Nature," the Goddess of the Sidhe. There is no denying the fact that A.E., like Robert Kirk, operated within the cultural parameters of his time. So he conceived of the ultimate divinity as the paternal Lir, and of Dana (or Sinan) as the "veil of Lir"—or deity viewed externally as the primal form of matter. However, Lir is seen as uniting all pairs and opposites—including male and female—within his depths, and can as easily be seen as the gynandrous Light/Dark Mother.

Dana, writes A.E., is "the basis of every material form from the imperishable body of the immortal to the transitory husk of the gnat." She is also the Divine Compassion; A.E. adds: "Her heart will be in ours when ours forgive." This same Goddess Dana was, in middle times in Ireland, also known as Brigid. And, as we have seen, Brigid's hidden presence may be felt behind the words of Kirk's *Secret Commonwealth.*

A.E. died in London, on July 17, 1935. His dictum had always been "Seek on Earth what you have found in Heaven." His life may be seen as an attempt to do just that: to bring our own world into closer contact with the world of the Sidhe—that first-manifested world of immortal youth from which we devolved long ago.

William Sharp

Our last great seer finds us in Scotland. Once again we find a mystery or, more accurately, a living myth—the myth of a beautiful, inspired woman living in the remote Western Isles of Scotland. "We were all under the shadow of the Fiona myth," wrote the poet W.B. Yeats.

However, the beautiful Fiona was not all that she seemed. It was not long before she was revealed as the alter-ego of the Scottish critic, biographer, and essayist, William Sharp. This revelation came as something of a shock to the adherents of the Fiona myth. Anyone less like the graceful Fiona than Sharp would have been hard to find. With his stout body, red face, and great crop of bristling hair, he represented the absolute antithesis of the fey creature of the legend. The general public response was laughter, a laughter in which even the usually sensitive Yeats joined at times. This was part of Sharp's tragedy.

William Sharp was born in 1855 and educated in Glasgow. He spent much of his youth among the Gaelic-speaking fishermen and crofters of the West Highlands, absorbing from them a great mass of Faerie lore. However, it was not until 1894 that he began to publish this material. From that date twelve volumes appeared in rapid succession under the name of his "dream-self," Fiona Macleod.

Fiona was much more than a literary device, a nom de plume; she was, in fact, a secondary personality—"as distinct a secondary personality as one reads about in books of psychical research," observed Yeats. When she "took over," Sharp was really, to all intents and purposes, a different person.

In his *Autobiography*, Yeats records several very interesting stories about Sharp which help to shed light on the mysterious symbiotic identity of William/Fiona. The first concerns one of Sharp's periodic bouts of mental anguish: Yeats was staying with MacGregor Mathers (then the leading light of the Hermetic Order of the Golden Dawn), and his wife, Moina, in their Paris appartment. One morning at the breakfast table, Mathers told Yeats of a vision he had had of a man standing in an archway wearing a kilt of the Macleod and another tartan. This news affected the poet strangely. He associated it instantly with Sharp and Fiona, and found his thoughts mysteriously drawn to them. Later, in the afternoon, he began to shiver violently, and sought Mathers' assistance.

Sharp must be in great need, he told Mathers. The occultist concurred: "It is madness," he said, "but it is like the madness of a god. "Apparently, however, only Moina Mathers could help in this matter. Yeats entered her room and instantly all thoughts of Sharp and Fiona left his head. "I have used a formula," explained Mrs. Mathers, "to send your soul away."

This story has an equally interesting sequel. Yeats later wrote to Sharp and ascertained that he had indeed been struggling with madness at that exact time. Yeats's soul, Sharp said in his return letter, had visited him in the form of a great white bird, and "Fiona" had also come to tell him he was healed.

Yeats also records the following story, told by Sharp himself to a somewhat uncomprehending audience. Apparently "W. S." (as Yeats referred to him) had been somewhere abroad, when he observed the astral body of "Fiona" enter his room in the form of a beautiful young man. At the same time he became aware that he was "a woman to the spiritual sight." "Fiona" then lay with him "as a man with a woman"—and for days afterward his breasts swelled up so that he had almost the physical appearance of a woman.

This mind-boggling account is, in fact, a perfect description of the sexual dynamics associated with "faerie lovers" (see Chapter Eight), but one can easily imagine the blank incomprehension and disbelief it elicited at the dinner table!

It sheds considerable light on the conundrum of William and Fiona. Apparently, Sharp himself conceived of "Fiona" as another being, and she proved to be as catalytic for him as the Queen of Elfland was for Thomas the Rhymer. If we compare

Sharp's account with the "Romance" of Thomas we can see that in both cases some form of specialized intercourse between a human and an Otherworld entity takes place. In the account above the polarities are reversed: William becomes the "woman;" Fiona, the "man." In other words, "she" takes over the impregnating role. This is exactly the magical sexual dynamic explored by Dion Fortune in her later novels, which feature as protagonists a strong initiating woman and a passive or "psychic" man.

That Sharp was aware of the dynamic, initiating nature of Fiona is apparent from the rather involved letter he wrote to Yeats, in order to explain their relationship. Or rather, "Fiona" wrote it to explain her relationship with her "friend" William. In this letter an allegory is used—that of the match, the wind, and the torch. "Fiona" is the match, initiating or catalyzing the process; William is the torch, burning brightly for all the world to see. The wind of the spirit blows between them, fanning the flames.

It is also clear that Sharp was an immensely gifted clairvoyant. Again, Yeats has an enlightening story. Ever the skeptic, the poet decided to test his friend "W.S." When the two men were out walking together, Yeats thought to himself, "When we come to the third bush, let us say, a red spirit will rush out of it." As soon as they reached the bush, Sharp stopped, perplexed, and said, "Some red thing has come out of the bush." The test was repeated, but Sharp always picked up on his friend's mental suggestions.

On another occasion, the two friends visited a faerie rath (hill). Yeats began an invocation. On turning to speak to Sharp, he could get no reply. "W.S." was, in fact, completely entranced, with his arms wrapped around a great elm tree. When he came to, he insisted that his soul had flowed in the sap circulating through the elm.

Whatever the abstruse astral mechanics behind the relationship of William and Fiona, there can be no doubt that it worked. In "her" books Fiona revealed a coherent body of lore which opened up the Faerie Way anew. There are enough hints in these marvelous works to enable the careful reader to work practically with faerie entities and experience firsthand the wonders of the Otherworld which they inhabit.

Fiona is at pains to stress that the Sidhe (known as the Shee'an or Sheechun in the Western Isles) are "great and potent, not small and insignificant beings," and in this she is in total agreement with our other seers. She points out that the Queen Mab of popular faerie romance is in fact the terrible Dark Queen, Maeve (Mebd, Medbh, or Mabh) of Scottish/Irish legend. As we have seen, the Dark Goddess is essential to the Faerie Way, and the dispenser of its most powerful initiations.

The bright or light aspect of the Goddess is not, however, forgotten in her pages. In Fiona's poem "The Love Song of Drostan," we read of "Dana, Mother of the Gods, moon crown'd, sea-shod, wonderful!... Like two flaming stars were her eyes/Torches of sunfire and moonfire..."

The essential unity of these two aspects is also stressed. It is one of the most potent keys of the Tradition.

Perhaps Fiona Macleod's greatest contribution to the restoration of the Faerie Way is her reinstatement of the Four Cities of the Tuatha de Danaan, or Sidhe, as its basic ground plan. We have already come across these Four Cities in Chapter One, where we examined the ancient Irish poem, "The Battle of Moytura." What follows is Fiona's beautifully poetic description of them:

> *There are four cities that no mortal eye has seen but that the soul knows; these are Gorias, that is in the east; and Finias, that is in the south; and Murias, that is in the west; and Falias, that is in the north. And the symbol of Falias is the stone of death, which is crowned with pale fire. And the symbol of Gorias is the dividing sword. And the symbol of Finias is a spear. And the symbol of Murias is a hollow that is filled with water and fading light.*

She went on, however, to give some tantalizing glimpses of one of the great secrets of the Faerie Tradition—the mysterious Fifth City of the Sidhe known as the Glen of Precious Stones. We will say no more of this now. Full instructions for visiting each of these Cities will be given in Chapter Seven.

Another major thread runs throughout all of Fiona Macleod's writings: the beauty and importance of our home planet, the precious Earth. This emphasis—which is also strong in Native American traditions—is particularly important for us today, as we face an ecological crisis of unfathomable proportions. In the following passage from "The Birds of Angus Og" Fiona provides what amounts to a Faerie "credo" in words highly reminiscent of the prophetic utterances of the Native American seer, Chief Seattle. She refers to the Faerie initiates as:

> *That small untoward clan, which knows the divine call of the spirit through the brain, and the secret whisper of the soul in the heart, and forever perceives the veil of mystery and the rainbows of hope upon the human horizons, which hears and sees, and yet turns wisely, meanwhile, to the life of the green Earth, of which we are part, to the common kindred of living things with which we are at one.*

However, the fruitful symbiotic relationship between William and Fiona was not without its drawbacks. Sharp paid a heavy price for the insight he gained. One aspect of this price was the periodic bouts of mental illness he had to endure. His footsteps were always dogged by that strange being known as Dalua, the Amadan-Dhu (Dark Fool, or Faerie Fool) "whose touch is madness and death for any mortal: whose falling shadow even causes bewilderment or forgetfulness." We have here the same motif as in the Thomas story of a meeting with a faerie woman leading to an encounter with the dark self.

Worn out by his struggle, Sharp died in Sicily in 1905. There is some evidence that his soul found repose beyond the gates of death. During the 1960s a medium in the south of England began to pick up messages, ostensibly from William Sharp himself. He now existed, he said, in a combined form with Fiona, as "Wilfion." The tension between the two identities, so fruitful and yet so unendurable, had finally been resolved.

It seems fitting to close this chapter with one of Fiona Macleod's greatest prophecies—a prophecy being fulfilled even now, and with an accuracy the equal of Thomas the Rhymer's.

Fiona looked forward to "a descending of the Divine Womanhood upon the human heart as a universal spirit descending upon awaiting souls." This would not occur in her own time. So she must speak to and for the future. She quotes in "Iona" the words of a young Hebridean priest:

> *As our forefathers and elders believed and still believe, that Holy Spirit shall come again which once was mortally born*

among us as the Son of God, but, then, shall be the Daughter of God. The Divine Spirit shall come again as a Woman. Then for the first time the world will know peace.

This "Second Coming" of the Divine Feminine is occurring as I write, not perhaps through mortal birth, but through an "immortal breathing upon our souls." It is the return of the Goddess.

CHAPTER FIVE

First Steps

The path into Faerieland lies open to all. It begins in the private mental space—the here and now of everyday experience—of any individual, and winds from there to the heights and depths of the universe itself. It is to this private mental space that we must address ourselves now. For if we are to embark upon the Faerie Way it is necessary to prepare our inner space, which is the true arena of our working. There are three important steps to preparing ourselves: relaxing, purifying, and energizing.

Being relaxed is of the utmost importance. None of the techniques outlined later in the book will work for you unless you are completely relaxed. This can easily be demonstrated by using the example of the dream machines currently so popular. The later programs for these, involving image and vision, can be successfully used only if the first level of relaxation programs have been completed. Otherwise, the brain is not susceptible to the state in which hypnagogic images appear. This state has been called by Robert Monroe, the researcher into out-of-body experiences, "mind awake, body asleep," and it is the cornerstone of any spiritual program.

Purifying yourself is also vitally important. Later we will learn how to see the patterns of the energy dimension parallel with our own. As a preliminary to that, we must first purify our inner space, so that we can see through and beyond the repetitive energy patterns that imprison us. This activity is rather like cleaning our mental windows so we can see out of them.

To attempt to see beyond the "normal" parameters of the mind requires tremendous energy. It is rather like paddling a canoe against a fierce current—you may even notice that you perspire quite a bit during meditation. This lost energy needs to be continuously replaced.

Breath Counting

Sit comfortably in a chair or, if you prefer, on a meditation cushion. Your eyes may be open or closed. Gently direct your mind to focus on your breathing as you count each breath. Each complete cycle of inhaling and exhaling equals one count. Count ten full cycles and then return again to one. Keep repeating this. Allow the counting to completely absorb your mind. If any thoughts occur, simply let them be—neither welcome nor shun them. They will fade of their own accord.

After you have become accustomed to this counting, begin to put some of your attention into the out-breath. Continue to count, and as you exhale, breathe out all of your tensions and irritations. Completely let them go. Soon your limbs should begin to feel pleasantly heavy—a sign that you are indeed becoming relaxed. Continue to count slowly from one to ten, from one to ten....

Try this exercise for short periods at first (five to ten minutes should be sufficient) and gradually work up to a longer time (from half an hour to an hour). It is particularly good to practice counting the breath first thing in the morning and last thing at night. Above all, experience what it is like to be fully relaxed. Your body will remember the feeling.

Dana Purification

In this visualization exercise we will work with the image of Dana, the Mother aspect of the Faerie Triple Goddess (Brigid being the Maiden; Morrigan, the Crone). Dana is particularly important here because she represents compassion, which is the most effective cleanser and purifier of all.

Always begin with a relaxation exercise as detailed above. Count each breath and completely release all tension. When you have become completely relaxed, visualize the Goddess Dana in the space in front of you. Dana sits upon a seat of stone in a summer meadow brilliant with marigolds and poppies. Behind her are rich fields of corn. Her golden hair streams out like rays of sunlight and she holds ears of corn tenderly in her hands. Her robe is a bright, rich red, and she is surrounded by animals, birds, and fishes. Immediately in front of her is a huge grail filled with blue, sparkling water.

As you visualize Dana in this way, pray to her with all your heart, in your own words, for purification and cleansing. You can also ask for her help on any matter that troubles you. Dana responds to your prayer. Her face is illumined by a smile of unutterable kindness and compassion. She directs streams of light from Her body into yours: white light flows from Her forehead into yours, clearing any impurities relating to your body; red light streams from Her throat into yours, cleansing the faculty of speech; blue light flows from Her heart to yours, removing all obstacles and impediments of mind. Take time to visualize each of these streams of light in turn until you feel truly cleansed and renewed by them.

You now notice that the grail at Dana's feet is overflowing with precious nectar. Feel this nectar washing over you, filling every cell of your body with vibrant new life.

Finally, the image of Dana begins to shrink, and rises until She is just above your head, facing the same way as you. Slowly it descends to your heart center, where the Goddess has Her true home, and dissolves into your heart. Rest for as long as you wish in the feelings of bliss and oneness that this union generates. You may like to ponder A.E.'s beautiful words: "Her heart will be in ours when ours forgive."

Repeat this purification whenever you feel the need. It is especially valuable before any magickal work.

Body of Light Energizer

After completing the relaxation and purification exercises described above, you are ready for the third and final stage of preparation: energizing. Begin by visualizing a sphere of brilliant white light just above your head. This sphere should be a little smaller than your head. Let yourself rest in this visualization for a few minutes. Really feel that the sphere is there.

Next, become aware that the sphere is slowly decreasing in size until it is only about an inch in diameter. When it has reached this size, it begins to descend through your head and body until it reaches your heart. From your heart the sphere of light begins to expand again until it encompasses your whole body. As it grows, it changes the substance of your physical body into pure light. Your skin, flesh, bones, and internal organs are all transformed. You have a body of light.

Rest in this state for as long as you can.

You may also visualize the sphere of light beneath your feet and raise it to your heart center in the same way. This is a good practice if you wish to attune yourself to a sacred site, as you are raising energy from the Earth Herself.

For at least the first month of practice you should engage in only these three methods (see Work Schedule, Appendix Three). Later you may use them as needed before any other working.

With these exercises, the purification of one's inner space is completed. The next stage of training involves creating harmony between this inner space and the outer world. It must be recognized that the distinction between inner space and outer world is essentially a provisional one. At this stage of the path it seems to us that there is a distinction and we act accordingly. The harmonization of inner and outer is thus very important. At a later stage of the path (we hope) we will come to the realization that our private mental space and the external space of the world were never really separate or different, but for the moment, for practical reasons, we can assume a difference.

The harmonization of inner and outer is effected by meditation on the four directions, which are also the four elements that make up physical matter, the four ages of human life, and the four seasons. By meditating thus we unite ourselves with the totality of life on this planet. Fiona Macleod expresses this great dance of the seasons and directions poetically:

Wind comes from the spring star in the East, Fire comes from the summer star in the South, Water comes from the autumn star in the West, Wisdom, silence and death come from the winter star in the North.

The four stars are the cosmic roots of life on Earth, and we will be repaid for befriending them. The following meditation is perfect for this purpose.

Prayer of the Four Stars of Destiny

For this prayer you will need a compass to establish the four directions. Once you are oriented, seat yourself centrally within the four points.

As before, begin by counting your breath until you are totally relaxed. Next, purify your inner space through the visualization exercise. Then raise energy with the Body of Light Energizer, as described above. Now stand and face the East. Be aware of a soft spring wind blowing from this direction, fragrant with all the scents of the season. Let it play upon your face. Say aloud:

Reul Near, Star of the East, give us kindly birth.

Think of your own birth, and of its circumstances. Think of all those thousands of beings who must enter the gate of the East this day. What sort of conditions will they meet? Think also of your eventual rebirth. This is the gate through which you will reenter the green world, when the time comes. Be aware of any seeds of new thoughts, new projects, in your consciousness. Let the spring wind play upon them and enfold them in its fragrance.

Next turn to the South. This time feel the warm South wind blowing upon your face. It brings the fragrance of a thousand flowers from summer meadows. Say aloud:

Reul Deas, Star of the South, give us great love.

Think of any time in your life that you experienced love in all its purity and strength, maybe the enveloping parental love of your first years, or the overwhelming feelings of a first affair. Relive the experience now. Think also of the many beings in the green world—and in other worlds—needing love, wanting love, worthy of love. Let your love expand to meet them. This is the gate of marriage and maturity, so think about these things as well. Anything in your life which you wish to grow and prosper should be caressed by the South wind.

After resting in the South for a while, turn to the West. The West wind is rich with the scent of autumn leaves and a faint taste of the sea. Say aloud:

Reul Niar, Star of the West, give us quiet age.

Think of your own advanced years, whether they are with you now or yet to come. Think of the word "quiet" in the prayer: every being in every world is entitled to a quiet age. Think of the benefits age brings in its train; for example, the opportunity to turn within in quiet contemplation. Every situation and being in your life that has achieved an extended span of years should be touched by the salty tang of the West.

Finally, face the North. The wind here is cold, with a flurry of snowflakes. Say aloud:

Reul Tuath, Star of the North, give us death.

Fearlessly face your own death. It will come to you from the North. Do not be morbid, but face the certainty that your life will end. Think of the thousands of beings who will leave the green world by the Northern gate before this day is through. Think of your own encounters with death thus far in life. What have you learned from them? Any situation or person you need to release should be passed through the purifying and bracing North Wind.

This meditation on death is not the end. Briefly face the East again as you close the prayer, in token of the beginning of a new cycle. See all the seeds of newness that you need to enrich your life. Sit for a while in silence, and close. There is no need to dismiss the powers of the quarter, any more than you would dismiss

God or Goddess at the end of a prayer. You have not commanded their attendance; you have befriended their power.

By performing this exercise, you lay the groundwork for experiencing the Four Cities as described in Chapter Seven.

We have seen that the faerie peoples are denizens of an energy realm contiguous with our own earthly plane. In the next exercise we will try to sense that energy realm, the Faerieland enfolded within our world's heart. We will try to see the lines of light that connect every object in the material world with its invisible counterpart in Faerie. Essentially, Faerieland is the perfect pattern—the matrix—from which all life on Earth flows and unfolds. This vision has many names: A.E. called it "The Many-Colored Land," while the Yaqui Indian shaman, Don Juan, expended much effort to enable his apprentice, Carlos Castaneda, to see these "lines of light."

The Many-Colored Land

For this exercise you will need a candle, which must be placed on a table, or your altar, so that you can see it easily. Light the candle and sit comfortably, gazing upon its flame. Count your breaths until you are absolutely calm. Now, half-close your eyes so that you can see the candle flame veiled by your eyelashes. You will see a multitude of lines of light reaching from the candle flame to your eyes. Slowly raise your eyelids, and, as if by magic, the network of light lines will draw back into the flame. Repeat this several times, and then conclude your meditation by counting your breath again.

The next stage of the exercise involves using what you have seen with the candle flame in an imaginative way. If you can go out into nature, so much the better. Choose a particularly beautiful spot, perhaps in a park, and sit there quietly. (If you really cannot get out into nature, try placing potted (uncut) flowers and shrubs upon your altar or table.) Now look at the bushes, flowers, and trees around you and see them surrounded by the same branching network of light lines; that is, transfer the vision you had with the candle to the natural forms around you. In time you will be able to see the light lines without imagining them, but for the moment you will have to use your imagination. Do not strain in any way; just let the light lines be there. Watch them withdrawing into and extending from the natural objects before you. Do not expect anything more. Just watch the light lines for as long as it is comfortable.

Practice this exercise as often as you can, but take care not to strain your eyes. Do not gaze for long periods without blinking, for instance.

When you can see the light lines easily, you may notice certain changes; the lines may shimmer, move, or pulsate, for instance. You may even see small humanoid forms moving through their web. These are the "small clans of the Earth's delight" (as Fiona Macleod called them), entities that are representations of the energy-forms of plants and flowers. Whatever happens, just accept it. Remember to always conclude your periods of "seeing" with a period of counting your breaths.

This exercise prepares you to meet your Co-Walker in Chapter Eight. Do persevere with these preliminary exercises. If you perform them well, your experiences with the methods outlined later in the book will be real and transformative. As with any spiritual path, the effectiveness of The Faerie Way depends on the groundwork of its initial stages. It is like the beginning of a faerie tale: the cows must be milked, the wood cut, and the sheep attended to before the prince or princess (in lowly disguise, of course) sets off for the enchanted castle.

CHAPTER SIX

Animal Helpers and Faerie Allies

No one begins a spiritual path, or reaches its culmination, alone. This truth needs to be strongly stated in the face of the individualism—even selfishness—which infects much New Age thought. It may seem to the aspirant as if he or she is alone, especially early in the journey, but when the end is reached it will be readily apparent that this was never the case.

In the Faerie Way we recognize our interdependence from the outset by calling on helpers or allies. Such helpers fall into two main categories: animal and faerie beings. Our belief that these beings are separate from us is a conceptual convenience, not a metaphysical truth.

We begin with the animal helpers, or "power animals" (as they are called in shamanic traditions). There has been much confusion about exactly what these creatures represent. We can say, as a preliminary definition, that they are the same beings as the spirit helpers of our Western healers and mediums, but they appear in animal form.

Why should this be? Our society, for many thousands of years, has focused mainly on human-to-human interchange as a means of learning. Just think of the dialogues of Plato, the cornerstone of Western philosophy. But other peoples—including our own ancestors—have long lived not only closer to nature than we have, but in fruitful symbiosis with it. We could say that they listened to the voices of nature. So while our guides tend to be human, their guides have a tendency to manifest in an animal form.

However, considering the current ecological crisis, maybe we in the West need to learn a little more from our animal friends. The Faerie Way offers us just that opportunity, revealing how our own culture once existed in a much closer relationship with the natural world. In contacting our animal helpers, we are in fact reconnecting with our deepest roots.

We are used to very solemn spiritual masters who utter pious (and wordy) homilies about abstract concepts such as "love" and "duty." Animal teachers are not like that, as anyone who knows the antics of the Native American tricksters Coyote and Raven will agree.

They jest, they caper, and above all, they teach primarily through symbolic action rather than words. Your animal teacher will probably present you with a series of symbolic visions. Discerning their meaning will be up to you. She/he may also lead you into cathartic situations in which fears and energy blockages are released—usually with a dose of rather dark humor!

Meeting Your Animal Helper

The technique for contacting your animal helper is actually very simple. Sit comfortably in a straight-backed chair. Do not use the yogic cross-legged position for this exercise. (Some people prefer to lie flat on their back on a bed or a mat during this exercise, although you may find that you drift off to sleep in this position. Experiment to see what works best for you.) Close your eyes and practice your relaxation exercise until your body and mind are rested and at peace.

Visualize before you now a cave or similar opening into the Earth—perhaps the hollow trunk of a tree, a pit, or a well. Allow this image to become strong and stable, and then walk toward and eventually into it. Do not try to see yourself doing this as if you were watching a character in a movie; instead strive to actually be there, walking and sensing your surroundings.

Once inside the cave, you will be met by a Guide, who may take one of many forms. She/he may be perceived simply as a shining, moving light, a gray-bearded ancient, or even an animal. If the Guide does assume an animal form, be sure that this is not your animal helper, but a companion to take you to the inner realm.

In the depths of your cave or opening is a tunnel reaching into the bowels of the Earth. The Guide now accompanies you through this tunnel. You may feel a sense of rapid acceleration as you travel. If so, do not be alarmed; this is quite natural and normal.

Eventually you emerge, with your guide, into an inner landscape. Just take some time now to acclimatize yourself and look around. What sort of landscape is it? Are there trees, mountains, rivers, lakes? What time of day is it? Is it cold or warm? Is it windy or still?

When you feel reasonably "at home," it is time to explore. Your Guide will wait for you until you return. Your objective is to look for an animal (or animals) in this landscape. Take note of any animals you see, and do not discount them if they are tiny and seem insignificant. Many would prefer a magnificent wolf, bear, or lion as an animal helper—perhaps not realizing that one of the most powerful animals in the Native American tradition is the humble mouse!

In classical shamanism one should see one's animal helper three times and from three different angles. However, you may prefer to trust your instinct as to which animal is right for you.

Obviously, you should avoid any animals which present bared fangs to you. They will act not as helpers, but obstacles on your path. When you have seen an animal which seems to have an affinity for you, be ready for any teaching it may wish to give.

If it has not already approached you, wait awhile and see if it will.

What happens next is not for me to tell you. Your animal helper may interact with you in any one of a thousand ways. When you feel that the experience is over, simply bid your animal farewell, and return through the tunnel with your Guide.

When you bid your Guide goodbye at the cave mouth, see before you your familiar room and gently merge with your body there. Take a few deep breaths, move your arms and legs, and open your eyes. Soon after you have fully "awakened" to your normal surroundings, it is a good idea to make brief notes detailing any visions or symbolic objects presented to you by your animal.

Now that you have acquired an animal helper who will accompany you on many of your future inner journeys, there are some things you may wish to do that will make your experience even more meaningful. One useful activity is to draw, sculpt, or model your animal. Even if you do not consider yourself an artist, you will find that any image you can create will be a source of power in your life. Even a crude "stick animal" will work wonders. Such an image can be placed upon your altar or within your meditation area.

Next, learn everything you can about your animal. If it is a wolf, for instance, find out something about the present distribution and condition of wolves in the wild. See if there is anything you can do to help, via animal charities or conservation groups. It is a good idea to offer something back to your animal for its help and service.

People who live in shamanic societies often spend a great deal of time observing their animal helpers in their natural state in the wild. In order for you to do this in a modern Western society, a little ingenuity is required. Television wildlife films offer an excellent opportunity to see your animals in a free environment. (Observing animals in captivity is not a good idea, as their behavior is severely modified by their confinement.) The importance of such observation cannot be overstated. Sir Laurens Van Der Post writes:

> *Watching the animals of the wilds makes you realize that there's obviously a kind of communication, a kind of aware-*
> *ness that we've lost. As an animal can assess situations*

from far away simply by smell, so our intuition is our sense of spiritual psychological smell.

Though our access to wild animals is, sadly, limited, we can watch their domestic cousins. And, conveniently enough, one of the most important animals of the Faerie Way is the dog. Other important animals in the Tradition, such as the butterfly and the bee, also offer little impediment to observation. However, if your animal is a bear or a wolf you will have to take up some of my suggestions above.

However you plan your observation, work with your animal frequently in the inner journeys in this book. Listen to its input. Soon you will find that your own sense of "spiritual psychological smell"—though long atrophied through lack of use—will return.

This is the great gift of animal helpers: they invite us back to the natural world from which we have long excluded ourselves. And that natural world is our true home.

Though we have already acquired an animal helper, we will need another spiritual friend—the faerie ally—to accompany us to the cities of the Faerie realm. Many of the observations related to the animal helper apply to the faerie ally as well; for instance, our faerie ally will also communicate with us through symbolic action rather than through words. We can also expect them to employ a few tricks or pranks to make sure the message gets across.

There are a few important points to understand before you meet your ally. Most important is that you realize that faeries are not merely imagined constructs of our inner world; they are real entities obeying the laws of their own world. Therefore, remember to treat them with courtesy and respect. You must also be cautious of them, for they possess formidable powers. Not all faeries make good allies; as Robert Kirk mentions, the *geirt coimitheth* (joint-eater or just-halver) attaches itself to a person and devours the essence of all that he or she eats. Consequently the individual affected remains as thin as a rake, no matter how much food she or he consumes.

So exercise great discrimination in the choosing of a faerie ally. Faeries themselves get a great deal out of the ally relationship and many will present themselves to you as prospective candidates when you signal your intent, so choose carefully. If you have even an inkling of a bad feeling about choosing a certain faerie being as an ally, then err on the side of caution and reject the candidate.

Also, remember that you do not have to choose any of the candidates. Think of this process as a job interview: if there is a poor turnout, the position will have to be readvertised.

How will you know when you have found your ally? It is largely a matter of attraction and intuition. Your will feel drawn to the right candidate in a subtle harmonic of sexual attraction. Note the word "subtle" here; the individual presenting himself or herself may be manifesting as either physical sex (or even in an indeterminate form) but the "inner tingle" you feel when in this faerie's presence will be like that which you would feel in a romantic encounter in the physical world. If this "spark" is not present, reject the prospective ally.

Along with this resonance of attraction goes an intuition, an inner feeling, that this is indeed your ally. Both of these factors should be present before you accept any candidate.

A word may be in order here about the appearance of the faerie beings. You have read A.E.'s descriptions in Chapter Four of this book, and these may be said to represent the perfect, classical faerie forms. Do not expect the beings that you see to be exactly the same. Faeries are great shapeshifters. They may appear to you in a somewhat bewildering array of forms—from the tall, shining princes and princesses of the Sidhe to beings of unprecedented strangeness.

Remember too that the form adopted by the faeries is their accommodation to our limited perception. In essence, they are beings of swirling, coruscating energy. Our perception of them is a sort of "freeze-frame" of this energy-flow.

One final point before you meet your ally: The elemental beings, which Fiona Macleod calls "the small class of the Earth's delight," make up only one small subdivision of the Faerie realm. These beings (known as devas in theosophical thought) correspond quite closely to the popular image of the faerie as a small winged figure hovering over the hedgerows. However, they do not make good allies for our purposes. Essentially, they are harmonics or echoes of the princes and princesses of the Sidhe, and they are comprised within their being. Only for certain specific magickal purposes—when an imbalance needs to be corrected—is an alliance with them deemed worthwhile, or necessary. We are aiming closer to the fountainhead of elemental energy, before it has become diversified into various forms, so for now it is wise to leave the "small class," lovely as they are, alone. With these provisos in mind you can now journey in search of your ally.

Finding Your Faerie Ally

Sitting comfortably as before, count your breath. Relax. See before you a lush green meadow. Feel the soft, wet grass on your feet and legs. On the horizon you see a low green mound. You head toward it, feeling a gentle breeze on your face blowing from the direction of the mound. Butterflies flutter in the air before you and you can hear the liquid song of the skylark and the caw of crows. Be aware of all the sights, scents, and sounds of the countryside.

As you reach the mound, you notice that it is about sixty feet long. You look around for some means of entrance into its depths. Though you walk around it, looking intently for an opening, you see no way in. Suddenly, however, your eye is drawn to a circular area in the side of the mound which is a different shade of green. Looking closely, you can see the reason for the change of color. Moss of a deep emerald green is growing amid the grass. Feeling with your fingers, you realize that the circular area is actually a door which swings back if you tug at it. This is the moss door. Open it and pass within.

Once through the moss door you find yourself in a tunnel of densely packed earth sloping abruptly downward. The tunnel keeps the same circular shape as the door. As you move through this tunnel you notice something peculiar—although there is no visible source of light, it is not totally dark. Light seems to be coming from somewhere, perhaps seeping from the very tunnel walls.

After a while this tunnel ends in another circular door, this one of weathered oak. Strange convoluted patterns are carved in its surface. This is the wooden door. Open it and pass within.

Now the tunnel walls are of damp and glistening rock. You see that steam seems to be rising from them, and you are aware of deep subterranean rumbles echoing beneath you. Still there is a faint light which enables you to see. You press on as the tunnel slopes and turns ahead of you.

Ahead of you now is a third door, circular like the others and made of white gold. A strange pattern rather like two schematic trees is cut into in its surface. As you look in amazement, the trees seem to move in a sinuous dance. The door itself seems to be melting and moving as if it were white hot. Here you must take your courage in your hands. This is the metal door. Open it and pass within.

What you will find beyond this third door I cannot tell you. Faerieland is different for everyone. However, at some point in your journey you must call your prospective faerie allies to you if they have not already appeared. Use all your powers of judgment in choosing an ally and remember—you do not have to choose any of the candidates. When the time seems right, return through the three doors to the green world. Note that the metal door may look different from within Faerieland. Mark its position well before you set off.

This method of the three doors for entering Faerieland is ancient and extremely powerful. You may use it whenever you wish. Even after you have gained a faerie ally, the three doors may still have much to show you.

Suppose that you have found an ally and later wish to end the relationship. What should you do? The following technique may prove beneficial in such circumstances.

Breaking Faerie Contact

Sit quietly. Count the breath for a while. When you are totally relaxed, visualize your unwanted faerie contact standing immediately before you. Now take an iron knife and rest its point just above your ally's head. Here you need to combine real and imagined space as seamlessly as possible. With the ally's head as north, now move your knife from North to East to South to West to North, completely circumscribing the faerie being. By doing this you are signifying that faeries too are bound upon the Wheel of Life and are subject to its changes. Remember Robert Kirk's words about the faerie tribes: "They remove to other lodgings at the beginnings of each Quarter of the year, so traversing until doomsday."

The movement of your knife is a symbolic reminder of this. And of course, the metal iron is hated and feared by the faerie tribes.

As you trace the circle with your knife, visualize the faerie being getting progressively smaller, until, just before your knife reaches North again, it has become a mere speck. As the knife completes the circle, all that should be left is pure, clear space. Rest in this space for a while. It is helpful if you can keep your eyes open throughout the exercise.

If you have chosen well, however, you should not need to break the contact. Both your animal helper and your faerie ally should become your true spiritual friends. Essentially, you will be a working team and perhaps even more than that. For the trinity of animal, faerie, and human is a reflection of that great primal unity from which we devolved eons ago. In the final analysis, your faerie ally and your animal helper are parts of your self long-lost, which had surfaced only occasionally in dreams or reverie, but are now together again as they were at the dawn of time.

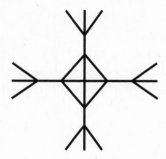

CHAPTER SEVEN

The Four Cities

With the winning team of animal, faerie, and human assembled, we are now ready to set out on a great adventure: the journey to the Four Cities of the Faerie Realm. Essentially, as we have seen, these cities represent node points of the wisdom-energy of the elements. As we visit them in turn we are, in fact, constructing a magick circle, both within the psyche and in the outside world. The completed circle or mandala can be regarded as a lens through which the powers of the universe become concentrated and focused.

The mandala, through the harmony of inner and outer worlds, encircles the entire planet. As we work to construct it our meditation room becomes the world itself; we invite all the world's diversity into our work area. This is why you will notice echoes of other peoples and lands and other faiths in the following workings.

The Faerie Way is not narrow and insular. We have already seen something of the importance of union with the land in the story of Thomas of Erceldoune. The time has long passed when such a union could exist with only a particular land or country at the expense of others. Now, "union with the land" means union with the planet in its entirety.

In the journey to the Four Cities we weave the Faerie mandala into the very fabric of the planet. Before we begin it must be understood that there is much more to the Four Cities than the information I provide in the following visualizations. The visualizations are a key, a means of entry only, and you must explore the Four Cities for yourself once the door has been opened. Once you have learned the basic sequence of images, you are free to go your own way and explore their byways and side streets. Build on what I have given you; do not content yourself with it. Give your imagination free reign.

A Journey to Gorias

First, establish the four directions as you did before the Prayer of the Four Stars of Destiny. Mark the East, for this is the direction we will travel today. Sit comfortably, facing East. Close your eyes and count your breath until you are fully relaxed. Become aware of your body and its solidity. Let your consciousness touch briefly on all its internal processes: circulation, digestion, heartbeat, brain function, etc. Next, be aware of any emotion you may be feeling. Simply note that you are feeling a particular emotion (if you are). Do not enter into the emotion. Let it go. Finally, be aware of your thoughts. Think of them as numerous boats passing under a bridge. You are situated on the bridge watching as they pass underneath. Just watch them without being tempted to jump into one. Let them go by.

After a while you find that you are separate from yourself and looking at your seated body from behind. Do not be alarmed at this; simply accept it. Look around the room. Can you see it clearly with your inner eye? Take note of the position of furniture, pictures, windows, and doors. Has the room changed in any way?

Now find yourself slowly drifting up until you are near the ceiling of your room. You can see your body beneath you, sitting quietly. You drift up through the ceiling, which offers no resistance to you. Now you are above your house, looking down at the roof. Still you are gently floating up, up into the sky. The town, village, or city in which you live lies spread out beneath you, and you can feel the first cool wisps of cloud caressing your spirit form.

Up through the clouds you float, and suddenly you are above them looking down on the shining white cloud castles illumined by the sun. Remembering the directions, you head due East, flying faster than any airplane, in the warm sunlight.

After you have been traveling for what seems only a short time, a sense of inner knowing tells you that you are near your destination. You swoop down like a bird, and through the clouds you can just make out glimpses of great ice peaks glinting in the sun. Going lower yet, you can see a mountain valley surrounded by rock towers like the pipes of a great organ. Still lower, myriad window-like openings are apparent in the rock towers. They must be inhabited, you think.

You can make out the valley floor now, a vibrant green with flower-jeweled gardens; trees and fields of golden wheat. Waterfalls cascade down the vertical rocky sides of the valley, running into a broad stream on the valley floor. You touch down now, by the side of this mountain stream. Looking up, you can see the ice peaks in the background, and hundreds of small square white buildings clinging to the cliffs, almost as if they were growing from the solid rock. A bracing breeze is blowing, fluttering through the many white pennants you see on poles among the houses. At the far end of the valley is a larger building, cubical like the stone houses, but with balconies and a glittering golden roof. This is your destination. But before you set off you must call your animal helper and faerie ally, if they are not already there.

The three of you set off, following the stream to the golden-roofed building. People are working in the fields; some of them stop to give you a cheery "hello." All around are more white flags and other curious wind devices which look something like prayer wheels. You pass many white houses, in which people can be glimpsed going about their daily tasks. Take some time to explore now.

The glory and profusion of flowers in this valley has to be seen to be believed. Blue poppies nod in gardens, and you can see the fuzzy petals of the edelweiss and the vase-shaped blooms of gentians. It is a ravishing feast for the senses. The air is crisp and clear with an invigorating tang and the sky is a deep, almost violet, blue. The stream sings merrily at your feet.

You reach the golden-roofed building, and find that its great wooden door lies open as if you are expected. Entering, you find yourself in a dark corridor which ends at another open door. You pass through this door into a large room which is entirely covered with magnificent, colorful paintings and hangings. Here you can see images of many-limbed monsters embracing each other in sexual union, fierce and ascetic saints, faeries of unearthly beauty, and terrible goddesses in rampant and ecstatic dance. All of these images are woven into the bright tapestry of nature with densely wooded hills, waterfalls, golden fields of corn, and snow-covered mountains. You feel that the entire universe is contained within this room and remain for a while in deep contemplation of these images. Note how each image in the paintings keeps its own form, yet is subsumed into the whole.

Your faerie ally breaks your reverie by touching you gently on the shoulder. Motioning to you, he or she raises one of the hangings to reveal a hidden door. You push the door gently and it opens. Passing through, you find yourself in a dim, smaller room, lit only by the golden radiance of its extraordinary central statue. This statue, of pure gold, standing on a small black plinth, is the only object in the room. You look closely at the form—a man with a drawn sword in his right hand. He is dressed like a prince, with an elaborate headdress. In his left hand is a long-stemmed flower. As you gaze upon his face, you are awed by its expression of utter peace and repose. Something makes you reach out and run your finger along the figure's golden sword. As you touch it, a jolt, almost like an electric shock, thrills through your entire being. It is as if the sword in your mind has been unsheathed, and you experience a sense of unprecedented clarity and stillness.

As you emerge from this blissful state, you look up and there before you is Esras, the teacher of Gorias. (Esras is from Celtic tradition, but this teacher has many names and can appear in either male or female form.) Listen now to the teaching to be given to you.

When your audience with Esras is over thank him or her, return up the stream, and bid your animal helper and faerie ally farewell. Rise once again into the air and fly homeward. Soon you will see the familiar surroundings of your native land beneath you. Let yourself sink down, down, through the clouds, through the roof of your house, through the ceiling of your room, until you stand behind your seated body as before. Then step forward and merge with your body. Take a few deep breaths, stretch, and orient yourself in the familiar surroundings of your room. You may like to stamp your feet emphatically on the floor to indicate that the journey is over. Then take brief notes of your adventure.

A Journey to Finias

Sit comfortably facing south, for this is the direction we shall travel this day. Proceed as you did for your journey to Gorias until you find yourself once more above the clouds. This time, however, travel due South.

Once again a sense of inner knowing tells you that you are nearing your destination. The clouds below you melt away and you find that you are traveling over a vast desert, with yellow sand dunes baking in the hot sun. You are rapidly approaching what appears to be an oasis, with silver-gray trees somewhat like poplars, and a cluster of ancient buildings. A road leads from the oasis, only to peter out in the desert sands. Spanning this road is a massive, cyclopean stone arch.

You touch down immediately in front of the great arch and call your faerie ally and animal helper. Together you look up at the arch, which is inscribed with numerous strange scenes and ancient writing. Passing underneath it, you proceed into the desert city.

Adobe houses, blinding white in the strong sunlight, flank your path. All around is the hard glitter of the silver green leaves of the poplar-like trees. Beings are in the houses and the streets and once again you are greeted cordially. You know intuitively that this is a place of perpetual light. There is no night here.

Now the silver-gray, slender trees are interspersed with date palm and eucalyptus. And the mysterious road from the desert ends at a great building composed of massive stone blocks. This building is in a state of complete disrepair. Great white stones are scattered beneath its walls as if the builders abandoned the project halfway through. A sense of mystery hangs in the air. What is this place?

You can make out huge, bare windows in the building before you and see that its massive wooden door stands open. Again, you feel that you are expected. Entering through the door, you find yourself in a long corridor with a floor of densely packed earth. Doorways lead off on both sides of the corridor. It is blissfully cool here, sheltered from the hot glare of the sun.

You enter through the first doorway and find yourself in a curious room. A bare oblong window looks out over the eternal desert. And in the floor—again of beaten earth—is etched a complex spiral pattern. As you step into the spiral you feel an irresistible urge to dance. It wells up within you, starting as an itchiness in your feet and spreading upward in waves. You cannot deny it. Slowly at first your feet begin to move, tracing the spiral path in measured tread. Then your hands are raised, almost against your will, and you begin to whirl, moving faster and faster around the spiral.

As you dance you become one with the movements of the stars. The earth floor disappears and you are turning, turning in deep space. Your being is filled with the song of the stars, the great shout of joy of the whole creation. Now you are whirling down to earth again, dancing into other beings, other lives. Fragments of these other lives weave themselves into the dance. You are male and female, young and old, black and white, all religions, all creeds—and none. You are the One becoming the Many. You are legion.

Now the ecstatic dance subsides and you find yourself once more on the earth floor. Your faerie ally touches you lightly on the shoulder and signals you to come with him or her. You follow, out of this room and into the next room in the stone corridor. This room has no window and is empty save for a wooden staff planted in the center of the floor. You contemplate the wooden staff for a spell, and notice green branches snaking out from its smooth surface. Buds in turn break out upon the branches, and as you watch in amazement, beautiful creamy-white blossoms burst forth from the buds. The staff is alive. A delicious and subtle scent fills the room.

You reach out to touch what is now a small tree. And as you do, something of the endless light of Finias awakens in your soul. As you raise your eyes you see Uiscias, the teacher of this city, standing before you. Be receptive now to any teaching he or she may wish to give.

When your session with Uiscias is at an end, thank him or her and return up the road and through the archway. Bid your faerie ally and animal helper farewell and begin your homeward journey. This will be exactly the same as the return from Gorias. As before, you may stamp your feet to signal the end of the journey, and then take notes.

A Journey to Murias

Proceed as before, but this time face West and journey in a westerly direction. As you descend through the clouds, you notice that they are gray and swollen with rain. A few drops spatter in your face. Immediately below you can see the wide expanse of the cold green-blue sea lit by the rays of the setting sun. The city of Murias lies between rounded green-brown hills and the sea. You see a cluster of tiled roofs surrounding a central hill on which stands a great cathedral with soaring spires and flying buttresses. Trees dot the hill, surrounding the cathedral with the deep reds, vermilions, golds, and browns of autumn leaves. Toward the sea there is a harbor, and you see a forest of masts. Many great and proud ships are berthed there, and there is a flurry of activity as cargoes are loaded and unloaded.

You touch down in a narrow cobbled street running from the harbor to the central hill. Here there are many shops with windows and bright displays of merchandise outside. However, it is just beginning to rain and some of the shopkeepers are hurriedly dismantling their displays and bringing them indoors. Again, some of the people exchange a cheery greeting with you.

Now it is time to call your faerie ally and animal helper. Together you proceed up the street.

The cobbles are slick with rain now, reflecting the light of the setting sun. The street is quite steep, and as you turn back momentarily you can see the busy harbor and the sea beyond. The smell of the ocean is in your nostrils and you can hear the raucous cries of gulls squabbling.

The street ends at the central hill, which you and your companions now climb. There is a little path among the autumn trees which winds to the great western door of the cathedral. At the door you pause again and look down upon the glistening roofs of Murias and the great encircling sea. Then you enter into the darkness within.

The cathedral is built of the same red stone as the rest of the dwellings in Murias. As your eyes adjust to the dim light, you see great branching pillars of stone, almost like huge redwood trees, ending at an intricate maze of fan-vaulting at the ceiling. Strange carved stone figures peer out at you with leafy, leering faces and ancient, wise eyes. The silence is almost palpable. There appears to be no one in the building but you and your companions.

At the east end of the cathedral of Murias is a great rose window, with a low altar before it. The rose is dark now, catching only the faintest light of the setting sun from the West door. You wish, wistfully, that you had seen it in full sunlight. Suddenly, as if in answer to your wish, the rose window is ablaze with light. The light is so strong that you have to shield your eyes for a moment, but you can soon make out a central point within its radiant blaze. From that central point the rose is unfolding. Petal after crimson petal unfolds from the germ of light. Is this stained glass or is this a real rose blooming before your sight? You cannot tell. You only know that you sense an inner unfolding, like a pleasing pang at the heart center, which is absolutely real. You watch entranced as the great rose of light blooms and grows.

Eventually the light fades and you come to yourself. Your faerie ally touches you gently on the shoulder and motions you forward to the low altar before the rose window. There is only one object on the altar: a slender chalice of beaten red gold. It is so beautiful, like the calyx of a flower, and the perfect symmetry of its form speaks to you of some lost harmony of the soul. You run your finger about its rim and feel again that pleasant pang at the heart, followed by a rush of tingling warmth. Standing before you is Semias, the teacher of Murias, smiling gently. Open now to the wisdom of Semias.

When you feel that the time is right, thank Semias, bid farewell to your companions, and journey home as usual. Again, end the session by stamping vigorously, and then take notes.

A Journey to Falias

Begin the procedure as usual, but this time face North and journey North. When you descend through the clouds, total darkness envelops you. For a while you are completely disoriented. The darkness is palpable and clinging and whichever way you turn you can see nothing.

Suddenly a great peal of thunder rings out and a jagged flash of lightning illuminates the clouds. Then there is darkness again. The thunder continues as you journey on doggedly, but each time, the lightning that follows it illuminates only thick, drifting clouds.

You wonder where Falias can be, and almost feel like giving up in your attempt. Then suddenly, far away, you can make out bright lights. They are stationary, unlike the sporadic wildfire of the lightning. You journey toward them. They grow larger and brighter as you approach, until the intensity of light almost dazzles you. Closer still, and they are revealed as slender towers of some metallic substance, each with a great shining crystal crowning it. Each crystal tower is pumping light into the encroaching blackness. A great joy fills you as you gaze at them. They are homing beacons for the soul.

You fly between the towers and all at once the city of Falias in all its golden splendor is spread out beneath you. It is as if all the cities of the green world—New York, Paris, Tokyo, London, and many others—have been combined into one. More accurately, this is the original, the archetype on which all earthly cities are modeled. It stretches across the horizon as far as the eye can see. Here are skyscrapers, bridges, rivers, parks, temples, cathedrals, and mosques, all shimmering with a golden light as if the very stones from which they are built were pure gold.

Swooping lower you skim over the broad streets and tree-lined boulevards. The cobbles and paving stones shine with the same mysterious inner light but there are no people or vehicles in sight. This great city seems to be entirely deserted. You pass a park, which is similarly empty of people. The trees are bare of leaves and yet the filigree pattern of their branches is inexpressibly lovely in the golden light. Although bare and empty, all of Falias is magnificently alive. Its beauty, its truth, is ancient, essential, pared to the bone.

Now you touch down in a broad street with tall, dignified houses. Something about these houses is strangely familiar, as if you are connected to them by poignant memories of some other life. The trees in this street are also bare, yet you have seen them before, when they were covered with green leaves and blossoms. You have seen these streets covered with the thick drift of autumn leaves; you have seen them filled with people. And you have known the people who lived here. A flood of heartfelt memories is unsealed in you and for a while, you remain in quiet contemplation.

Now you call your animal helper and faerie ally. Together you proceed up the street. All the streets of Falias are arranged in a pattern of radiating spokes converging upon a central plaza in a wheel-like pattern. It is to this central plaza that you must travel.

At the very heart of the city is a great block of meteoric rock which fell from the stars at the very dawn of time. As you approach, you notice that this stone is also crowned with a golden radiance, a flickering nimbus of light playing around its surface. In its presence, you find your flood of memory is renewed and augmented and you think back to a time before time when the stars and your soul were young. There are strange memories now— memories of other worlds, other beings, strange landscapes.

You are roused from your reverie by the touch of your faerie ally who signals to you that you must touch the stone. You reach forward and as your hand makes contact with the black, shiny surface, something changes inside you. Something of the ancient wisdom of Falias awakens in your soul. You have traversed this Wheel of Life many times; you remember. Feeling now that someone is standing behind you, you turn, only to find yourself confronted by Morfesa, the teacher of Falias. Feel yourself open now to any teaching Morfesa may wish to give you.

When Morfesa signifies that it is time for you to leave, thank him or her, and return to your touchdown point. Say goodbye to your animal helper and faerie ally, and return home as usual, once again flying through the thunderstorm that surrounds Falias. Stamp to indicate the end of the journey, and take notes.

Make these journeys initially on four consecutive days of the week. After you have done this you may like to combine all four journeys in one session to get a sense of the interplay between the Cities and the turning of the Wheel.

As you visit each City you can add a symbolic object to your altar: a sword or knife for Gorias, a spear or staff for Finias, a cup for Murias, and a stone or crystal for Falias. These are, of course, the so-called "magickal weapons," but in my view this conception is an inheritance from the dominative, manipulative warrior mentality of the last four thousand years and is best avoided. Look at your objects simply as symbols of Nature's power, not as weapons to force Her to do your will. In any case do not use iron for your objects. A soapstone letter opener will be perfect for Gorias, and a wooden staff or even a small potted tree for Finias. Iron is inimical to the faerie peoples.

For some of the later work in this book it is necessary to energize all Four Cities. Once you have made the initial contact and explored a City at least cursorily you may energize it by simply visualizing its symbolic object in the appropriate quarter. This opens yourself to its power.

Above all, do explore the Cities. You may think I have given your animal helper and faerie ally little to do in the above highly schematic workings. Believe me, if given the opportunity, they will take you, via some very interesting byways, to other powerful centers in the Cities. Each journey you make will increase the power from the appropriate quarter by making the Cities more real for you. Follow your companions, take your time, linger. You are exploring your own soul and it has many wonders to show you.

The Prince of Tír-na-Nóge

Deidre at the Door to Her Dun

The Spirit of the Pool

A Warrior of the Sidhe

The Stolen Child

CHAPTER EIGHT

The Realm of Faerie

The journey to the Four Cities empowers us for other adventures in Faerieland. It is now possible to take a faerie lover as part of the process of spiritual growth. This is not a path for everyone; of all the exercises in this book, the following is the only one that is entirely optional. If you feel any hesitation at all, it is best to leave it alone—at least for now. Yet there is no doubt that this is one of the most powerful methods of pathworking of all for those so inclined.

Literature is full of accounts of those who have taken faerie spouses. There is the story of the Ulster Warrior Cuchulain who was offered Fand, wife of the sea god Manannan MacLir, to be his own wife if he would fight with the hosts of Faerie. There is also the tale of Ossian, enticed into Faerieland by a woman of the Sidhe; and the departure of the Knight Lanval for Avalon, in the Norman "lai" of Marie de France.

On the whole, however, faerie lovers have received bad press. They have been persistently portrayed as fickle, sexually demanding, and even dangerous. "As for the incontinence of the Leannain Sith (faerie lovers), or succubi who tryst with men, it is abominable," fulminates the Reverend Robert Kirk. And William Grant Stewart in his book, *The Popular Superstitions and Festive Amusements of the Highlanders of Scotland*, has the following coy passage:

> *The faeries are remarkable for the amorousness of their dispositions, and are not very backward in forming attachments and connections with the people that cannot with propriety be called their own species.*

Such views may be misleading. Wentz records a charming story which gives a contrary position: a Scotsman named Lachlann was in love with a faerie woman. Eventually he became tired of her and began to fear her approaches. Things came to such a pass that he decided to emigrate to North America. As soon as this plan was fixed in his mind, women who were milking at sunset out in the fields heard the faerie woman singing:

> *What will the brown-haired woman do
> When Lachlann is on the billows?*

However, Lachlann's plan of escape did not work, for the faerie woman followed him to Cape Breton, Nova Scotia. She would not relinquish her love.

Here, it is the human partner who is fickle. The faerie woman, by contrast, demonstrates great and steadfast love. But there is a warning here against taking faerie marriages lightly. Lachlann found that even the ocean between them could not quench the ardor of the brown-haired woman's passion.

Why, then, should one take a faerie lover? We have seen that faeries represent and embody the enlightened energy of the elements and directions. Union with a faerie being is thus a union with the wisdom-energy or primal force of creation. In a sense, such a union can be considered the end of the spiritual quest. The Welsh wonder tale of Kulhwch and Olwen is primarily an account of a trip to Faerieland to find a Faerie wife. After all his trials and tribulations, Kulhwch wins such a wife—Olwen—and his quest is concluded. In the Tibetan dakini teachings, the dakini consort guides the aspirant inexorably toward enlightenment.

So our faerie lover can be our guide to the consummation of enlightenment. But this process, once it has been initiated, cannot be halted.

We have seen how Thomas of Erceldoune was irrevocably changed by his union with the Queen of Elfland. In just such a way will we be changed by meeting our faerie lover. However, before we come to the working, a few guidelines must be given— and these must be rigorously observed in order that we may move safely through a complex and subtle experience.

First, realize that this will be a real experience involving contact with a real being. As I have said before, faeries are not merely imagined constructs or even Jungian archetypes, but actual entities in their own real world. It follows, then, that real commitment will be required of us—and all the courtesy, tact, and honesty that we would bring to a relationship in the everyday world.

The second point is more subtle: although faeries are real beings, our natural habitat is not in their world. We strive to bring their primal enlightened energy through to our own world. We do not want to get stuck in theirs. This is why after his seven years of service with the Queen of Elfland, Thomas of Erceldoune returned to his own country. The green world of common experience is his true home, and it is here that he must use the Queen's gifts. Only at death can he return to the primal energy world of Faerie to be renewed and refreshed.

We must, therefore, keep a grip on our own world at all times. One way to do this is to be aware of both worlds at once. We have seen that anyone can manifest the Faerie energy at any time. Therefore, as we explore the relationship with our faerie lover we should look for reflections of that energy in the everyday world. Our normal partner may embody this energy for us at particular times, and we can become aware of this. Or, if we have no partner at present, working with a faerie lover can draw such a one to us. Above all, it is imperative not to get "stuck" in the relationship with our faerie lover, lest we end up like poor Lachlann, haunted even to the ends of the Earth. The two worlds are really one, and are separated for the sake of logical convenience only. Manage the energy flow in the everyday world and all will go well.

This is a difficult concept to grasp, because the relationship of the Faerie world to our own is one of mutual projection. The faerie peoples mirror us and we mirror them, but on both sides of the mirror are real people and not mere reflections. To concentrate on one side of the mirror at the expense of the other is to block the energy flow between them (the "stuck" experience). Just as if our faerie lover and our Earthly lover were the two poles of a magnet, when both are in place the energy flows between them and all is well.

What this means in practice is that if you do not have a physical partner and do not intend to work with one in the future, skip the following working. Otherwise, a dangerous imbalance could occur.

Finding Your Faerie Lover

Sit comfortably and count the breath until you are fully relaxed. Energize each of the Four Cities in turn. Remember, this is done by visualizing the symbol of each city in the appropriate quarter: a sword for Gorias in the East; a spear or staff for Finias in the South; a cup for Murias in the West; and a stone or crystal for Falias in the North. As you have already entered Faerieland by the three doors method given in Chapter Six, there is no need to repeat this now.

See before you now a green meadow, lush with all the flowers of spring. You walk through the meadow feeling the softness of the grass on your bare feet. The sky is a cloudless blue and the soft breath of a warm breeze plays about your face.

Ahead of you is a low hill crowned by a magnificent flowering hawthorn tree. You climb up the banks of the hill and seat yourself with your back to the trunk of the tree. Looking up, you can see the deep pink of the blossoms with their delicate white stamens moving in the breeze. A penetrating, musky scent fills your nostrils. Rest here now, peacefully.

At some point your faerie lover may approach you on your left side. When this happens, if it happens, allow the experience to unfold. Remember this is a courtship, so be attentive, courteous, and tactful. You must be sure of the rightness of the contact, so if you have any apprehension or unease about the being who has come to you, give your thanks and return immediately to the green world. If the contact feels right, just relax and enjoy the experience. Your faerie lover may take you on from this point deeper into Faerieland. Always request that she or he bring you back to the rendezvous point by the hawthorn tree before you return to your own world.

When you feel that the time is right, bid your faerie lover farewell and return through the meadow to the green world. You can always meet your faerie lover again at the same place in the future.

Finally, de-energize the Four Cities by visualizing their appropriate symbols diminishing in size and finally disappearing. Stamp your feet vigorously and take notes.

Do not let the simplicity of this technique mislead you. Its power resides in the symbol of the flowering hawthorn which acts as an inner beacon, a declaration of your intent. You may even do the exercise by a real hawthorn tree in a secluded spot, with equally powerful results.

If you should ever wish to break off contact with your faerie lover, simply use the technique given at the end of Chapter Six. It will work just as effectively in this context.

If you have worked through all the exercises thus far in the book you may already have some awareness of the presence of your inner teacher. He or she may have appeared to you during your journey to the Four Cities or been with you in Faerieland when you encountered your ally. However, if you have not encountered such a being as yet, the following exercise is designed for you. Your inner teacher may be one of the four great seers of Chapter Four—this is especially likely if you felt particularly drawn to one of the personalities while reading this material. Or he or she may be one of the great unknown teachers of the tradition. It really doesn't matter. As long as you feel happy with your teacher, this is all that counts.

Meeting Your Inner Teacher

Sit comfortably as before and relax, counting your breath. Energize the Four Cities. Become aware of your body, emotions, and thoughts in turn, as in the journey to the Four Cities. Next see yourself standing behind your body, observing it. You walk out of your house, leaving your body sitting peacefully as it is, and into the street outside. Look at the front door of your house and see if you can see it clearly. Observe the vehicles or people in the streets, the weather, the position of the sun or moon.

Now imagine the air around you changing to water. You are at the bottom of a great ocean and you float up, up toward its surface. As you journey up, paddling with your hands, you can see light shining through the water, becoming stronger, until at last you break the surface into glorious sunlight.

You tread water, getting your bearings. Far away you can see the shore with a line of white cliffs and foaming breakers. You swim for the shore with firm, energetic strokes. Soon you reach the white sand and look up at the high cliffs. A narrow path winds up the cliff's face. Climb this now. As you climb you may hear your name called from below. If so, do not look down but carry on purposefully until you reach the summit.

As you climb over the top of the cliff, you see before you a great plain of emerald-green grass stretching away to a range of great ice peaks in the distance. You must travel across this plain. Again, if you hear your name called, do not turn aside from your path. Ignore the voice and press on.

Soon you are in the foothills of the great mountain range. And there, nestled in a spur of the hills, is a small cottage, its door standing open. You are expected. You enter the cottage, and there waiting for you is your inner teacher. Spend some time with him or her now. There is much to talk about.

You have several choices now. In the cottage is a tiny temple or chapel. You may like to spend some time in meditation with your teacher there. Or your teacher may wish to take you further up into the mountains on a journey. However you spend your time, when you feel that the interview is concluded, bid your teacher farewell, and return by the same path—back over the plain, down the cliff (ignoring any voices), into the sea, swimming out, sinking down, down until you are outside the door of your house. Use your imagination again to transform the water back into air, and enter your house to merge with your sitting body.

Take a few deep breaths and open your eyes. De-energize the Four Cities, stamp your feet, and take notes. You may return to visit your inner teacher at any time by the same route.

Much has been said in the previous pages about the mirroring capacity of the Faerie peoples. In the next exercise we will meet our own mirror-image or "Co-Walker" in Faerieland. Speaking of this being, Robert Kirk says:

> *They call this reflex-man a* coimimeadh *or Co-Walker, every way like the man, as a twin brother and companion, haunting him as his shadow and is often seen and known among men, resembling the original, both before and after the original is dead.*

If we remember that Faerieland is the paradisal template of our own world, we can see the Co-Walker as the primal energy pattern from which our own life is generated. It thus has more claim to be called the "original" form than Kirk allows, not only outliving our own mortal body, but preexisting it as well. It functions much like the etheric body, by transforming energies from the unmanifest worlds into a manifest form. Contact with our Co-Walker, then, will align our own energy centers to the flow of energies from the "higher," original world. We have probably diverged from the original template of our lives many times and in many ways. We are "out of sync" with our real energy pattern. The following exercise steers us gently back to the authenticity of our pristine form.

Finding the Co-Walker

Sit comfortably. Count the breath until you are relaxed and then energize the Four Cities. Again, visualize the light lines, as you learned in the exercise "The Many-Colored Land" in Chapter Five. This time, however, see the light lines extending from your own physical form. Feel them branching out from your body and reaching out into space.

Imagine now that these light lines reach all the way to the borders of Faerieland. You can see Faerieland now with its sumptuous greenery and noble, ancient trees. Your light lines reach across the border, into the realm of Faerie, and there they join a shining being, one of the many whom you can see going about their tasks. The light lines connect you to this being. See him or her clearly now. You are seeing yourself in the pure mirror of wisdom, free from the dust of countless experiences. See the face of the being and look deep into the eyes. Now feel the power flowing to you through the light lines from the shining being, the primal power of the first manifested world in all its freshness. Feel that power irradiating and renewing every cell of your body.

The light lines are shining brilliantly now, forming a radiant golden connection stretching from where you sit to Faerieland. There is something musical about this light, as if the lines are resonating to the ancient (and yet ever-new) song of creation. The power continues to flow as you rest in the experience.

When you feel that the time is right, return your attention to your breathing. Do not mentally dismantle the lines, or imagine them retracting. Just leave them there and withdraw your attention from them. Take a few deep breaths, de-energize the cities, stamp your feet, and take notes.

You may find that you become aware of your Co-Walker at various times throughout the day and night. Just relax at these times and sense the energy coursing through the lines. Friends of a psychic disposition may even see your Co-Walker. Do not worry if this occurs; it is merely a natural consequence of increasing psychic growth.

By now you should be feeling quite at home in Faerieland with all the new friends and acquaintances you have made there. But it is time to press on. Two great initiations await you as we go deeper into Faerieland in the next chapter.

CHAPTER NINE

Deeper Into Faerieland

Thus far you have visited the Four Cities of the Tuatha de Danaan, acquiring wisdom and teaching. You have also, hopefully, gained a faerie ally (or allies) and an animal helper. In addition, contact with one of the inner teachers described in Chapter Four will have been made.

With this background work done, you should be in a strong enough position to undertake the two great initiations in this chapter. However, please bear in mind that they are initiations. If you go through with them, your life will change—in many ways.

No precise timing is given for these two workings in the work schedule (Appendix Three). Attempt them only when you feel the time is right; do not force it. Discuss this matter with your inner teacher, and be guided by his or her counsel.

Many people expend a great deal of energy contacting an inner teacher only to completely ignore the advice given when it conflicts with their current ego interests. Do not do likewise. No one expects you to completely abnegate your own will before your teacher, who is not, after all, an omnipotent guru figure; in fact, you may have many fruitful arguments with him or her. But at least consider the teacher's advice carefully.

One final point before we enter the Faerie realm again: these visionary sequences must be worked in the order given. You must visit the Glen of Precious Stones before you encounter the Washer at the Ford. Any amount of time, however, may elapse between the two experiences.

The Glen of Precious Stones

Complete the usual induction procedure by counting the breath for a few minutes. Then briefly energize each of the Four Cities in turn, starting with Gorias in the East. When you are satisfied that your circle is "alive" with power, become aware of your body, emotions, and thoughts as before. Soon you find yourself looking at your seated body. This time, however, we will not be traveling far. The path into the Glen of Precious Stones begins at your own front door.

Move toward the front door now, leaving your body sitting peacefully in its place. As you exit the door you notice immediately that something fundamental has changed. The familiar environment of your neighborhood has disappeared, and you walk out upon a high hill in bright moonlight. Above you the stars are shining brilliantly. As you look at them twinkling above they seem to be moving, wheeling about the central point of the heavens marked by the Pole Star.

This vision dazzles you, and you look down from the stars to take stock of your surroundings. From the vantage point on the hill you can see a wide valley winding away to the horizon. Upon the summits of the hills which enclose the valley you see watch fires burning, and you sense that the path is guarded. Far away on the horizon, where the valley seems to end, you can see a mysterious red glow, coruscating and glimmering with an unearthly brilliance. Within the rich ruby-red light you catch twinkles of all the other colors of the spectrum.

You know that this incandescent light marks the site of the Glen of Precious Stones, Fifth City of the Tuatha de Danaan, your destination. You descend the hill, feeling its soft, springy turf beneath your feet, and enter the valley.

Looking back, you can see your own house, perched on the summit of the hill, miraculously transposed into Faerieland.

Now, call your animal helper and faerie ally. They come willingly at your call, eager to be on this journey. There is a path winding through the valley, and by its side a little bubbling brook. The three of you set foot to the path of worn earth and proceed onward.

The dark hillsides which enclose the valley are thickly forested. Rustles and whispers of life come from the trees, which sway in a warm, gentle breeze. Occasionally, you are aware of the passage of an animal—perhaps a badger on its nighttime hunt for food—through the undergrowth near the path. A white owl drifts past on silent wings. All along, the sound of the little brook keeps you company.

It is altogether a strange sort of night, for sometimes the warm breeze seems to have in it a touch of winter coldness, causing you to shiver. Then it is warm again. You can see the trees nearest the path very clearly and you notice something curious: some of them have entirely lost their leaves and stand bare in the moonlight. Others are covered with white blossoms. Occasionally, you see apple and pear trees covered in fruit, while the leaves of a great oak nearby are a rich autumnal red. It seems as if all the seasons are mixed here, and you feel an atmosphere of timelessness around you.

Looking up, you can still see the watch fires burning on the summits of the hills. But the red glow is getting nearer now, entirely filling the horizon. Eventually you can see it as a soft, pulsating aura immediately ahead of you. It blocks your path, filling the entire valley, and you can see within it exploding scintillas of multicolored sparks chasing each other in mad play. Just a few more steps and you will be within the ruby glow.

You remember your intent and firmly step through. All at once the world changes. The entire landscape is irradiated with red light; the darkness of the night has disappeared. As you look in wonder you see that the trees have changed, too: they are made of living crystal with leaves of emerald and tourmaline. The path beneath your feet is composed of masses of precious and semi-precious stones. You are walking upon diamonds, topazes, beryls, and agates. Even the rocks in the little brook have become great amethysts, radiating their own inner light.

An owl flies by and alights on a huge boulder of black jasper. With some amazement you see that its body and wings are composed of gold-brown citrine crystal, and it has glowing garnets for eyes. There are other animals and birds, too, each formed from living gemstones. You find that you can see the life force flowing in their veins and arteries as a liquid ruby fire.

If you are challenged at this point by any being, your faerie ally will vouch for your good intent, but you must proceed further into the Glen. You see that it is formed in the shape of a great heart, and at its exact center you find a great fountain of light bursting up from the jeweled earth. This fountain is of an even deeper and richer ruby color than the surrounding glow. It gushes up joyously, seeming to reach the very stars themselves.

As you watch, the great and beautiful beings of the Sidhe approach the fountain in ranks and immerse themselves in its radiance, one by one. They are tall, with shimmering robes and flowing hair. Some wear great cloaks of many colors, caught with intricate brooches. Others carry tall lances whose points glimmer in the light. As they enter the fountain you see their forms illumined by electric ruby fire. They drink and breathe in the light, smiling with pleasure at this influx of the life force. As they leave the fountain, the light is still playing around them in endless configurations.

Now it is the turn of your faerie ally. He or she steps forward into the fountain to feast on its light. Your companion animal follows suit. Both return to you radiant and shimmering, and you realize that it is your turn. You step forward into the gushing light and feel yourself renewed by its electric fire, which penetrates every atom of your being. Color becomes sound and you are permeated by the great song of joy of the first creation.

As you step from the fountain you realize that you have been renewed in the most primal springs of life itself. You vow to bring this light to the green world when you return, and give thanks to the Sidhe for the great privilege they have granted you.

Now, rejoin your faerie ally and animal helper and retrace your steps back to the green world. Bid them farewell at the base of the hill and climb up to where your house still stands, miraculously, in Faerieland. Open the door, enter, and you are back in the everyday world. Merge with your sitting body, take a deep breath, and open your eyes. De-energize the Four Cities, stamp your feet, and take notes.

The Washer at the Ford

Count the breath until you are relaxed. Now energize all Five Cities of the Tuatha de Danaan in the following sequence: Glen of Precious Stones, Falias, Gorias, Finias, Murias. The Glen should be visualized as a column of ruby fire reaching from the earth beneath where you are sitting to the sky above you. Really feel that this column reaches from the very center of the Earth to the stars. Energize the other Cities as you have before, by visualizing their symbols at the appropriate directional points.

Now see before you a stone archway with a stout oak door. Make this door as real as you can. See its heavy metal latch. Then, step forward and open the door. You find yourself on the first step of a stone staircase which spirals into the bowels of the Earth. Despite the darkness ahead, you begin to descend, feeling your way. The walls feel damp and cool and you cling to them as you continue your descent. After what seems like an age in the darkness, your hands suddenly feel a wooden surface ahead of you. It is another door. You fumble for the latch and upon finding it, open the door onto a wide seashore. You have exited through a doorway in a huge boulder. You wonder how such an apparently endless spiral staircase could be contained within a boulder. But remember—normal physical laws do not apply here!

You are on a vast expanse of white sand. In the distance you can see the sea, and hear the muffled boom of the surf. Gulls wheel in the blue sky above you, and their screams merge with the sound of the sea. A strong wind is blowing and cloud-shadows chase themselves along the white sand. You think briefly of your animal helper and faerie ally but do not call them. This is a path you must travel alone.

You walk on, past barnacle-encrusted boulders and ribbons of pungent seaweed. The day is bright, the sun is shining, and yet there is something oppressive in the atmosphere, as if a thunderstorm is building. High cliffs rise to your left as you walk along the beach. As you walk, you spy a little cove set into the cliff wall. This seems to be your destination so you enter the cove. At its end a waterfall descends the cliff face to a deep pool in the rocks. Water cascades over the edge of the pool, forming a river which flows away to the sea.

As you look, just for a moment you see a shadowy form on the rocks by the pool. It seems to be that of a woman washing clothes in the cascading water. You squint to see more clearly, but it is too late—the woman has disappeared, if indeed she was ever there. Maybe it was just a trick of the light.

The ominous feeling persists, though, and it is quite dark and somber within the high walls of the cove. Nevertheless you decide to bathe in the pool. Removing your clothes, you immerse yourself in the icy water. At first the shock takes your breath away, but then the effect becomes invigorating. It is as if you are washing away all the grime of the world. The seaweed at the bottom of the pool is velvety soft to your feet and you begin to relax.

Suddenly, a loud cry startles you. A large, glossy black crow is eyeing you from a nearby boulder. Sensing a disquieting intelligence behind its eyes, your sense of unease returns. Yet there is no malice behind the crow's eyes. It hops away over the wet rocks, occasionally turning its head to look back at you.

The cry of gulls is louder now, almost like the sound of a crying woman. You get out of the pool, dry yourself and find a warm, flat rock to lie on. A feeling of tiredness seems to have overtaken you. You close your eyes—and suddenly the crying noise of the gulls rises in a great surge. You look up, and see immediately before you a whirling in the air. It looks something like the circle made by an airplane propeller revolving at high speed, but some inner feeling tells you that this is the whirling sword of the Washer at the Ford.

It was she, perhaps, who appeared before in the shadowy shape of a woman and later as the figure of the crow. But you feel no fear. You remember the lucid, compassionate intelligence behind the crow's eyes.

The inner knowing is strong now. You know that you must walk through the swirling of that flashing sword. And you know that you will not be harmed if you do. Nevertheless, it is a terrible thing. You have read the old tales of the Washer and they are not pretty.

Steeling yourself, you take a deep breath and walk through the orbit of the whirling sword. There is no pain. But you are falling, falling, through black space. And you are different. Your body is gone; you are a diamond point of intelligence—the essence of yourself. All that is inessential has fallen away and you are your own pure individuality. It feels strange to be like this, but not unpleasant. Precisely the opposite, in fact—you feel liberated, freed, renewed.

Suddenly your fall is halted by a sense of pressure from above. For a moment this verges on unpleasantness and you feel anxious. Just then, the blackness around you opens out into a beautiful soft radiance. You are still that diamond point of intelligence, the essence of you, but now you are surrounded in that radiant, limitless space by innumerable other "diamonds." And, wonder of wonders, you can communicate with them, all of them, at once! You have access to all the wisdom and experience of the other diamonds. It pours into you, irradiates you. You have access to the knowledge of the Whole. Rest in this state for a while. Enjoy it.

You wish for this blissful state to continue, but the sense of pressure comes again, this time from beneath you. You are shooting upward, into the blackness again—a soft, velvety, encompassing blackness this time. And then you are in the light once more, the light of the seashore cove, as you awaken on your flat rock. You rub your eyes. Was it just a dream? But the crow is there, regarding you inquisitively, its head cocked to one side. You feel renewed and invigorated. The ominous feeling has gone. It seems only fitting to leave a present for the crow as token of appreciation for its gift of wisdom.

You reach into your pocket and find the perfect gift waiting there: a symbol of the encumbrances in your life which you have shed, both in the pool and in the deeper "dream." You set it before the crow, who picks it up in its beak and hops away. Once again, however, it turns to eye you compassionately as you leave the cove.

On the homeward way your steps are lighter. You bring with you back to the green world a new wisdom, a lightness, a streamlined sense of being. Find the door in the boulder now and return up the spiral staircase.

See the familiar surroundings of your room again and merge with your body. De-energize the Cities, stamp your feet, and take notes.

Now, whenever you begin a working you may energize all of the Five Cities. If you are working a circle, the Glen should be visualized in the exact center as a great column of ruby-red fire and light joining Earth and Heaven. Its symbolic object is a ruby, although a less expensive stone such as rhodochrosite can be used instead. One way of preparing your working space is to place your five symbolic objects in the characteristic Faerie mandala form (see Figure 4) and sit centrally, either holding the red stone representing the Glen, or with it resting on the ground beneath your feet.

The Fifth City may be worked in situations that require regeneration and renewal. It is especially useful in healing work. Visualize the person or persons to be healed within the column of ruby light, and see it working the alchemy of renewal within every cell of his or her body. Or you may wish to have the actual person stand or sit within the mandala as the Glen is energized. Another method is to "charge" a red stone within the column and then use it for healing work.

The pool in the cove of the Washer at the Ford may be used whenever you feel the need to shed something that is stifling your life. The Washer's, or Morrigan's, great function is to deprogram the destructive addictions in our lives. Return to the pool as often as you wish, but always travel alone.

These two initiatory experiences will take you deeper into the Faerie Way. But this is not a path that ends at some ultimate Nirvana. Wherever you are, whatever state you have reached, even deeper and more fulfilling experiences await you.

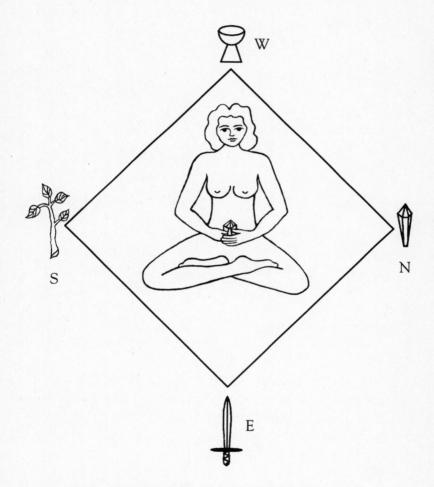

Five Symbolic Objects in the Faerie Mandala

FIGURE 4

CHAPTER TEN

The Future

We have seen how the Faerie Way, beginning in the remote mists of prehistory, was "reinvented" as a spiritual path by Victor Anderson and Gwydion Pendderwen in the 1960s. Their work in turn inspired Starhawk's *The Spiral Dance* (1979), a book which influenced an entire generation of pagans and occultists. The Faerie Tradition is now one of the fastest growing varieties of paganism/Wicca in both Great Britain and the United States. Authors such as R.J. Stewart and Steve Blamires are expanding and deepening the tradition, and in Ireland—where there are those yet alive who remember the shining beings of the Sidhe—there has been something of a renaissance of the old Faerie Faith.

Why should this be? One reason stands out fairly clearly: our planet is on the verge of ecological collapse—its seas poisoned, its forests denuded, its animals and birds ruthlessly slaughtered. We all realize that something is terribly wrong, and the source of that wrongness seems to lie in the way we have been thinking about the natural world for the last four thousand years. The Faerie Way offers an antidote to the selfish, dualistic thinking which has led us to the brink of planetary disaster.

The Faerie teachings provide us with an image of our world as a harmonious whole comprised of interpenetrating planes of energy. Some of these planes can be accessed with the five senses and the use of scientific instruments. Others are more subtle and intangible, but still very real. This vision offers us an ecology of the invisible; it allows us to work for the harmony and coherence of the whole by exploring the mysterious byways of our inner worlds.

There is something, say the teachings, that we can do now about the state of the planet. We can bring our own world, inner and outer, back into harmony with the radiant pattern of primal creation. We can bridge the abyss between our Earth and the Earth of Light, between this world and Faerieland.

In fact, Faerieland represents the original blueprint for planet Earth. The ego is the builder, but it has skimped on materials, cut corners, and ignored safety regulations. The result is the world we see around us, with all its imperfections and injustices. By going back to the original plans, we can begin, slowly, to rebuild our shattered world. Until fairly recently our world and the world of Faerie were in much closer communion. The shining figures of the Sidhe were still seen on mountains and near lakes, on lonely paths, and even occasionally in our villages and towns. The process that began with the Industrial Revolution effectively sundered the worlds. Now we who wish to do something for the planet have no more effective tools than those provided by the Faerie Way. By weaving the Faerie mandala about the planet, we weave the worlds back into primal harmony.

The Faerie philosophy is one of total interdependence. As Robert Kirk writes, "Nothing moves but what has another Animal moving on it, and so on, to the utmost minute corpuscle that [is] capable to be a receptacle of life." All creatures thus depend upon other creatures for their very existence, and no creature exists by and for itself as an independent entity. This is the teaching known as "egolessness" or "emptiness" in Buddhism, though it immeasurably predates the historical Buddha. If we bear this knowledge in mind we will be incapable of acting in a ruthless or exploitive manner towards our environment, for we will realize our total dependence upon it. "We" do not end at our fingertips; we flow out into the natural world and the power of the inner universe flows with us.

This is the great secret that the Queen of Elfland shows Thomas of Erceldoune: that he is one with the land and that the land's life is his own.

In just such a way, we are one with our own land, not in the sense of our narrow racial and geographical identity, but in the sense of being one with the planet itself. The land spoke through Thomas the Rhymer; the Earth will prophesy through us.

The Faerie Way, then, is not a way of selfish individualism. It works cleverly to loosen the ego's grip by showing us the shining realm that is our own birthright, the beauty that could exist on our own Earth. The Faerie vision of a peaceful world, a Faerieland on Earth, understandably attracts, and will continue to attract, adherents.

Other people may be drawn to the Faerie Way by the feeling that "something is going on" in the innumerable UFO contacts of the last forty years which cannot be explained by the extraterrestrial hypothesis. As we have seen, the UFO experience may simply be the current manifestation of the Faerie faith of our ancestors. The "visitors," as Whitley Strieber calls them, are here to teach us some hard lessons at this juncture of history—lessons about the "middle way" of balance between the polar forces which control our lives—which we must learn, or perish.

It is because we are so woefully out of balance that the visitors/faeries often appear to us in dark and disturbing forms. They wish us to learn to control our fear, and they wish us to see what a change that fear has wrought in the paradisal world. If we have the courage to see ourselves as we truly are, in the dark mirror of the visitors, we can then begin to change. Undoubtedly, we need to change, for we are now lost in darkness and our mother mourns.

We have begun the process of balancing by working through the exercises in this book. However, it is vitally important, if we wish to maintain the balance achieved, that we do not regard the information given in this book (or others of a similar kind) as some sort of dogma. "Pagan fundamentalism" seems to be one of the major pitfalls of the New Age. In fact, the Faerie Way can coexist as easily with Christianity or Buddhism as it can with Wicca. This point is essential to grasp if we wish to think of the future with any optimism. Religious intolerance has bedeviled the planet for over four thousand years and is still claiming lives at a sickening rate. As I have said, the Faerie approach is to "invite the world within your circle"—and that means inviting the world's many faiths as well. We can learn from all the Earth's religions, provided that we are not conditioned by them. To isolate ourselves in the "one true faith," to bar the windows and pull up the drawbridge to the outside world, is to commit spiritual suicide.

A similar caveat applies regarding the problem of identifying ourselves too strongly with any particular racial or national group. Much of the language and imagery of the workings in the preceding pages comes from the Celtic tradition. Yet I would not claim that this work in any way reflects a solely Celtic spirituality. To dress in the clothes and adopt the mores of a bygone historical era or racial group is to miss the point entirely. The Faerie Way is a universal spirituality, existing in many forms and in many lands. What I have tried to convey in these pages is the essence of the path.

Therefore, if you find techniques from other faiths which work for you, don't be a purist. Simply incorporate them into your work schedule. If you find, for instance, that the "Turn" or sacred dance of the Sufis fits well with the maze path or spiral pattern in Finias, by all means include it. Numerous techniques from the Christian devotional tradition might apply to Murias, while Tibetan teachings would find a home in Gorias. Search teachings out wherever they may be and incorporate them into the mandala of the Cities. You may revise and edit such teachings as need be, but keep their essence. Remember the words of the great Sufi teacher Rumi: "Do not look at my external form, but take what is in my hand."

This way, your mandala will begin to grow and, eventually, it will contain the world. Weaving the Faerie mandala about the world is equally a weaving of the world into your mandala. When you engage in this practice, you change inside. What was previously alien and external to you becomes close to your own heart.

You embrace the ancient wisdom which the Tuatha tasted at the dawn of time but which is now scattered like countless beads of mercury throughout the world's faiths and philosophies. You begin to speak with the voice of the land.

The future holds a great challenge for the human race: to create just such a universal mandala through which the ancient wisdom-energy can flow unimpeded. Our friends, mirror images, allies, and lovers in Faerieland are at work on this project and they ask us to join them.

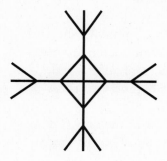

The Ballad and Romance of Thomas the Rhymer

The Ballad

(Collated from the Scott and Jamieson versions)

True Thomas lay o'er yonder bank,
And he beheld a lady gay,
A lady that was brisk and bold,
Came riding o'er the fernie brae.

Her skirt was of the grass-green silk,
Her mantle of the velvet fine;

At every lock of her horse's mane
Hung fifty silver bells and nine.

True Thomas he took off his hat,
And bow'd him low down to his knees;
"All hail, thou mighty queen of Heaven!
For your like on Earth I never did see!"

"O no, O no, True Thomas," she says,
"That name does not belong to me;
I am but the queen of fair Elfland,
And I am come here to visit thee.

"But ye must go with me now, Thomas,
True Thomas, ye must go with me;
For ye must serve me seven years,
Through good and bad, as may chance to be."

She turned about her milk-white steed,
And took True Thomas up behind,
And whenever her bridle rang,
Her steed flew swifter than the wind.

For forty days and forty nights
They waded through red blood to the knee;
And they saw neither sun nor moon
But heard the roaring of the sea.

O they rode on, and farther on,
Until they came to a garden green;
"Light down, light down, ye lady free,
Some of that fruit let me pluck for thee."

"O no, O no, True Thomas," she says,
"That fruit must not be touched by thee,
For all the plagues that are in Hell
Rest upon the fruit of this country."

"But I have a loaf here in my lap,
Likewise a bottle of claret wine;
And now, ere we go further on,
We'll rest a while, and ye may dine."

When he had eaten and drunk his fill,
The lady said, "Ere we climb yon hill,
Lay your head upon my knee,
And I will show you marvels three.

"O see you not yon narrow road,
So thick beset with thorns and briars?
That is the path of righteousness,
Though after it there's few inquires.

"And see ye not yon broad, broad road
That lies across yon lily leven?
That is the path of wickedness,
Though some call it the road to Heaven.

"And see ye not that bonny road,
That winds about the fernie brae?
That is the road to fair Elfland
Where you and I this night must go.

"But, Thomas, ye must hold your tongue,
Whatever ye may hear or see;
For if a word you should chance to speak,
You will never get back to your own country."

He's gotten a coat of the even cloth,
And a pair of shoes of velvet green;
And till seven years were past and gone,
True Thomas on Earth was never seen.

111

*The Ballad
and
Romance of
Thomas the
Rhymer*

The Romance

(Translated from the Thornton Manuscript, written 1430–1440)

As I went in days of yore,
Speeding my way and making moan,
On a merry morning in May,
By Huntley Banks, my self alone,
I heard the jay and the black bird,
The thrush sang plaintively her song,
A wood lark called like a bell,
So that all the wood about me rang.
Alone in longing thus as I lay,
Underneath a comely tree,
I saw where a lady gay
Came riding over a lovely lea.
If I told it until doomsday,
With my tongue struggling to say,
Certainly the lady gay,
Could never be adequately described by me.
Her palfrey was a dapple gray,
Such a one I never saw;
As does the sun on a summer's day,
That fair lady herself she shone.
Her saddle was of rounded bone,
Full seemly was that sight to see!
Stiffly set with precious stones,
And hemmed all round with emerald,
Stones of the Orient in great plenty.
Her hair about her head it hung,
She rode over that lovely lea;
She blew upon her horn and sang.
Her saddle girths were of noble silk,
The buckles were of beryl,
While the stirrups were clear crystal
All overlaid with pearls.
About the horse's breast were iral-stones,
The crupper was of goldsmith's work,
And as pure gold her bridle shone,
While three bells hung on either side.

Seven hounds about her ran,
A horn hung down about her neck,
And she had many arrows under her belt.
Thomas lay and saw that sight,
Underneath that comely tree.
He said: "This is Mary most mighty
Who bore the child that died for me—
But if I speak with yon lady bright
I fear my heart would burst in three!
Now shall I go with all my might
To meet her at the Eildon tree."
Thomas quickly arose,
And ran over that high mountain.
If it be as the story says,
He met her at the Eildon tree.
He knelt down upon his knee
Underneath the greenwood spray,
And said: "Lovely lady, have mercy on me,
Queen of Heaven, as you well may!"
Then said that lady mild of thought,
"Thomas! let such words be;
Queen of Heaven am I not,
For I never took such a high degree.
But I am of another country,
Though I be costly appareled
I ride on the hunt with my hounds.
They run at my command."
"As you are richly appareled
And ride thus in folly,
Lady, if you are wise
Give me leave to lie with you in love."
She said, "Man, that would be folly,
I pray you Thomas, let me be,
For I say to you truly
That sin will undo all my beauty."
"Now lovely lady, have mercy,
And I will dwell with you for evermore;
Here my troth will I plight you
Whether you believe in Heaven or Hell."

113
*The Ballad
and
Romance of
Thomas the
Rhymer*

"Man of mould! You will mar me,
Yet you shall have all your will;
But know it well, you will come off the worst,
For all my beauty will you spill."
Down then lay that lady bright,
Underneath the greenwood spray;
And, if the story tells it right,
Seven times by her he lay.
She said, "Man, you like your play!
What bird in bower may compare with thee?
You make merry with me all the live-long day,
I pray you, Thomas, let me be!"
Thomas stood up in that stead,
And he beheld the lady gay;
Her hair it hung all over her head,
her eyes seemed out, that before were gray.
And all the rich clothing was away,
that he saw before upon her form;
Her one leg was black, the other gray
and all her body like beaten lead.
Thomas lay and saw that sight,
Underneath that greenwood tree,
Then he said, "Alas! alas!
In faith this is a doleful sight,
How are you faded thus in the face,
That shone before as the sun so bright!"
She said, "Thomas, take leave of sun and moon,
And also of leaf that grows on tree;
This twelvemonth shall you with me be gone,
And Middle earth no more will see."
He kneeled down upon his knee,
Underneath that greenwood spray
And said, "Lovely lady! Have mercy on me,
Mild Queen of Heaven, as you best may.
Alas," he said, "and woe is me!
I believe my deeds will work me ill.
My soul, Jesus, I commit to thee,
Wheresoever my bones shall fare."
She led him in at Eildon Hill

Underneath a secret lee
Where it was dark as midnight mirk,
And always the water up to his knee.
For the space of three days
He heard only the sighing of the flood;
At last he said "Full woe is me,
Almost I die for lack of food."
She led him into a fair herb garden,
Where fruit was growing in great plenty;
Pear and apple, both ripe they were,
The date and also the damson,
The fig and the purple grape.
The nightingales were building their nest,
While parrots flew about
And thrushes sang without respite.
He reached forward to pluck the fruit,
Faint with hunger as he was.
She said, "Thomas, leave them alone,
Or else the fiend [devil] will attend.
If you pluck the fruit, truly I say,
Your soul will go to the fire of Hell,
There to remain until doomsday,
Eternally in pain to dwell.
Thomas, soothly, I call you;
Come lie down with your head on my knee.
And you will see the fairest sight
That ever saw man of this country."
Immediately he did as she him bade,
Upon her knee his head he laid,
For to repay her he was glad,
And then that lady to him said:
"See you now yon fair way,
That lies over yon high mountain?
That is the way to Heaven for sure,
Where sinful souls are past their pain.
See you now that other way,
That lies low beneath yon rise?
That is the way, truth to say,
Unto the joy of paradise.

115
*The Ballad
and
Romance of
Thomas the
Rhymer*

See you yet a third way,
That lies under yon green plain?
That is the way, with pain and trouble,
Where sinful souls suffer and grieve.
But see you now a fourth way
That lies over yon deep dell?
That is the way, truly to say,
To the burning fire of Hell.
See you yet a fair castle
That stands on yon high hill?
Of town and tower it surpasses all;
On Earth there is none like it.
In truth, Thomas, that is mine own,
and the King's of this country;
But I would rather be hanged and drawn
Before he knew that you lay with me.
When you come to this gay castle,
I pray you, be a courteous man;
And whatever anyone asks of you,
Take care to answer none but me.
My Lord is served at table,
With thirty knights fair and free;
I shall say, sitting on the dais,
I took your speech beyond the sea."
Thomas still as a stone he stood,
And he beheld that lady gay;
She came again as fair and good,
And also rich on her palfrey.
Her greyhounds were filled with deer's blood
She leashed her hounds
And blew her horn with might and main,
Unto the castle she took the way.
Into the hall softly she went,
Thomas followed by her side.
Then ladies came, fair and gentle,
Kneeling to her with courtesy.
Harp and fiddle played gaily,
Cittern and also psaltery,
Lute and rebeck rang out,

And all manner of minstrelsy
But most marvelous of all
As Thomas thought standing on the floor:
Fifty deer were brought in
That were both great and abundant.
Hounds lay lapping up the blood,
Cooks came with dressing knives,
And carved as if they were mad,
Revel among them all was rife.
Knights danced by three and three,
There was revel, game and play;
Lovely ladies fair and free
Sat and sang on rich array.
Thomas dwelled in that solace
Longer than I say, in truth,
Till one day, so have I grace,
My lovely lady said to me:
"Get ready, Thomas, to travel again;
For you may no longer dwell here,
Go quickly, with all your might and main,
I shall return you to the Eildon tree."
Thomas then said with heavy cheer,
"Lovely lady, now let me be.
For certain, lady, I have been here
No more than the space of three days."
"In truth, Thomas you have been here
For three years or even more;
But longer here you may not dwell,
The reason why I shall tell you:
Tomorrow, the foul fiend of Hell
Among this folk will fetch his fee,
And as you are handsome and strong,
I know full well he would choose thee.
For all the gold that ever may be,
From Heaven unto the world's end,
I would never betray thee
Therefore, I beg you, come with me."
She brought him again to the Eildon tree,
Underneath that greenwood spray,

117

*The Ballad
and
Romance of
Thomas the
Rhymer*

In Huntley Banks, where it's pleasant to be,
And birds sing both night and day.
"Far out in yon mountain gray,
Thomas, my falcon builds a nest,
A falcon is a heron's prey,
Therefore in no place may he rest.
Farewell, Thomas, I wend my way,
Homeward over the brown moors."

Pathworking the "Ballad" Sequence

When you have visited all Five Cities, you may pathwork the "Ballad" sequence above, if you wish. Read through the "Ballad" several times until you are thoroughly familiar with the imagery and the stages of the journey. Then sit down in your meditation place and quiet the mind by counting the breath. The next stage involves visualizing the story in as much detail as possible. You can either visualize yourself joining Thomas and the queen on their journey or become Thomas for the duration of this exercise. Whatever your choice, the following points must be noted:

1. Always start beneath the flowering hawthorn tree mentioned in the "Faerie Lover" exercise. This is the "Eildon tree" alluded to in the text, and an important rendezvous point on the inner planes. Lie beneath this tree and await the approach of the queen.

2. As you lie, be vigilant for a particular inner sound that signals the Queen of Elfland's approach. This sound resembles the tinkling of many little bells—the bells on her horse's mane—and is related to the sound of the sistrum in the Isian mysteries.

3. The queen will take you from the Eildon tree deeper into Faerieland. Jump up behind her on her white horse.

4. As you wade through the river of blood you may be overcome by a desire to sleep. Resist this as much as possible. The river marks a major change of consciousness as you leave the gravitational pull of the earthly body and it is best to remain aware as you cross it. However, if you do fall asleep, do not worry. With increasing practice you will be able to cross the

river in full consciousness. The duration of the crossing—forty days and forty nights—is symbolic, not actual, and is found in many other stories worldwide, for example, the account of Christ's temptation in the wilderness.

5. The eating and drinking of the bread and wine signals another change of consciousness. Enter into it fully and maintain your awareness. Remember, there is a warning against plucking the fruit. Do not ignore it simply to "see what happens."

6. The vision of the three ways may seem to conflict with the five ways given in the "Romance." However, the roads to Heaven and Hell are doubled up in the "Romance," leaving essentially the same three ways presented in the "Ballad." Take care to keep to the "middle" way, the bonny road to fair Elfland, the mean between extremes.

7. When you follow the bonny road, do not expect Elfland to correspond exactly to the description given in the "Romance." For the medieval author of the "Romance," Faerieland was a mirror of the courtly world of the middle ages, with its feasting, merrymaking, and minstrelsy. As twentieth-century men and women, our own perceptions may be very different. Just let Faerieland be as it is—for you.

8. When you wish to return, allow the Queen of Elfland to accompany you back to the Eildon tree. Bid her farewell, allow the vision of the tree to fade, de-energize the Cities, stamp your feet, and take notes.

The Avatasamka Sutra and The Faerie Way

They avouch that Every Element and different state of being, has [in it] Animals resembling those of another Element.

For it is one of their tenets that nothing perishes, but, as the Sun and Year, everything goes in a Circle, Lesser or Greater, and is renewed, and refreshed in its revolutions. As it is another [tenet] that Every Body in the Creation moves, which is a sort of life, and that nothing moves but what has another Animal moving on it, and so on, to the utmost minute corpuscle that is capable to be a receptacle of life.

—Robert Kirk
The Secret Commonwealth of Elves, Fauns and Fairies

The Indescribable—Indescribable
Turning permeates what cannot be described...
It would take infinity to count
All the Buddha's universes.
In each dust mote of these worlds
Are countless worlds and Buddhas...
From the tip of each hair of Buddha's body
Are revealed pure lands that cannot be described...
Nor can their wonders, glories, names and beauties

—From the *Avatasamka Sutra*
quoted in Garma C.C.Chang,
The Buddhist Teaching of Totality

Work Schedule

The following is just a suggestion for pacing the work program. After Month 5, you can undertake the two initiations in Chapter Nine and the Ballad sequence pathworking in Appendix One. At the end of the six-month period, it is probable that some of the exercises will have become firm favorites. Keep working at these, as you will be surprised at just how much they still have to offer.

Month 1

Daily: Breath Counting
Body of Light
Dana

Month 2

Daily: As Month 1, but add:
Prayer of the Four Stars
The Many-Colored Land

Month 3

Daily: As Month 1, but add:
Faerie ally
Animal helper

Month 4

Daily: As Month 1, but add:
Four Cities
The Many-Colored Land

Month 5

Daily: As Month 1, but add:
Inner Teacher
Co-Walker

Month 6

Daily: As Month 1

The Goddess in
Faerieland

If you have worked at the exercises in this book, you should have by now a living contact with the energy-realm around you. It will be apparent in all sectors of your life as a template or grid overlaying the green world and indicating instantly wherever an imbalance occurs. As you work to correct such imbalances you will realize the truth of the equation: the green world minus the shadow self equals Faerieland. The great writer George MacDonald (1824–1905) expresses this truth memorably in his novel *Phantastes*. Anodos, the hero of this work, muses after his trip into Faerieland: "Thus I, who set out to find my ideal, came back rejoicing that I had lost my shadow."

The following working continues this theme and also inaugurates a new work cycle. The Goddess in Faerieland will give you individual instruction on how to continue the great quest.

The Goddess in Faerieland

Sit quietly as before. Count the breath until you are relaxed and then energize all Five Cities. This is another solo trip, so you will not be calling your animal helper or faerie ally.

If you are not fully confident of your ability to see Faerieland, use the three door method of entry.

See yourself now on a wide green savanna. The sky above is a deep blue and the air is warm. The grass reaches to just above your waist and is cool and dewy to the touch. You press onward, and after a while you are aware of a flash of tawny color to your right. You see it again, just out of the corner of your eye, and then it disappears. Obviously you are being followed.

It is really warm now, even somewhat oppressive. You wipe your forehead and gaze up into the cloudless sky. Looking around you can only see the boundless savanna stretching for miles. There is no path.

Suddenly, there is a commotion around you in the grass and a great lion romps out in front of you, shaking its tawny mane. The lion roars ferociously and then sits upon its haunches, regarding you imperiously. You try to skirt by it but it invariably moves to block your path. It seems as if it is waiting for the answer to some unspoken question or a password. However, this is Faerieland, where all the animals have the power of speech. In a deep, rasping voice the lion asks you a question, which you must answer correctly in order to proceed.

You have answered the question to the lion's satisfaction, and now it joins you on your journey, padding along by your right side. On the horizon you can see a great forest and you sense that your path leads through it.

As you reach the outlying trees, you notice that night is falling. The moon has not yet risen and it grows very dark. You are deep in the forest now, which is lit only by a faint phosphorescent glimmer from the trunks of the ancient trees. It is like walking down the aisle of a great cathedral with the trees soaring above you in a canopy of fan-vaulting. The lion still lopes faithfully by your side. The silence is almost palpable.

You reach the shores of a deep, still lake in the center of the great forest. The lion squats on its haunches again and you sit also, worn out from the exertions of the day. Looking at the still waters of the lake, you see the reflection of the silver moon as it rises. Just then you hear the bellowing of a stag, quite near. The sound is mournful and spine-chilling and you look up from the lake's depths.

On the far shore of the lake is a great white stag raising its antlered head to the moon. The moonlight shimmers on its flanks, and both stag and moon are reflected in the deep lake. For a moment you catch your breath at the beauty of the scene. Then you get up and walk stealthily around the lake towards the stag.

As you approach, the animal becomes aware of your presence. But it does not startle and bolt; it simply regards you steadily with its deep red garnet-like eyes. You reach out a hand to pet its muzzle. It twitches slightly, but lets you caress the velvety skin.

And now the stag, the white hart of legend, has a question for you, which you must answer correctly in order to proceed. Listen carefully.

After you have answered correctly, the white hart trots after you as you return around the lake to your friend the lion. You wonder if the lion will have carnivorous designs upon your new companion, but in fact the two animals get on well together, nuzzling each other with pleasure. The lion's purr is so loud that it echoes through the glade.

You proceed out of the forest with your friends, the lion on your right and the white hart on your left. And now, once again you are in the outlying trees. You must have been in the forest for an entire night, for the sun is coming up, sending spears of light through the forest aisles.

You soon find yourself in beautiful open land with every variety of deciduous and coniferous tree. Great oaks spread their sheltering canopies in the dawn's light. Soaring pines stretch to the heavens. Now, ahead of you is a stone-walled garden, with a wide arch for a gate. As you look at the arch you can see a serpent slithering through the climbing ivy. Doves are flying all around with the pale light of dawn reflected from their white wings. Their cooing breaks the silence.

As you enter the arch, you are immediately aware of a maiden splendidly enthroned beneath a crystal coping at the far end of the garden. She wears a coronet of white flowers and the horned moon is upon her head. On either side of her are beds of deep pink roses. She is naked except for a white cloak with a deep blue inlay, which stretches to her feet.

Rabbits gambol around her throne, and birds are everywhere: hoopoes, pigeons and golden orioles resting on the flower-bejeweled grass. She is the one you have been seeking. She smiles a welcome at you and you feel emboldened to approach.

However, the white hart and the lion must approach first. They immediately take up their places beside her throne, the hart to her right and the lion to her left. You realize this is their natural place, which they have left to guide you to the Goddess.

The Goddess holds a pink chalice before her heart. Twin serpents twist about it, their tails entwined about the stem. She signifies that you must drink of this. You step forward and drink. And then the Goddess has much to tell you.

The draught from the chalice sends an electric tingling throughout your system. Your vision blurs for a moment, and when it clears you see that the Goddess has vanished. Beneath her crystal coping is now an oak door. You realize that the Goddess is a door. Pass through that door now into whatever landscape you find. Mark the position of the door well, for you must return through it when your journey is over.

When you return through the door you find the white hart and the lion awaiting you. They will return you to the green world. (You do not need to pass through the forest this time.) Bid them farewell, merge with your body, de-energize the Cities, stamp your feet, and take notes.

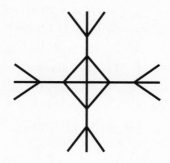

Bibliography

A.E. (George William Russell). *The Candle of Vision*. Dorset: Prism Press, 1990.

_____. *Song and Its Fountains*. Burdett, NY: Larson Publications, Paul Brunton Philosophic Foundation, 1991.

Allione, Tsultrim. *Women of Wisdom*. Harmondsworth: Penguin/Arkana, 1986.

Baring, Anne and Cashford, Jules. *The Myth of the Goddess*. Harmondsworth: Penguin/Arkana, 1993.

Barrie, J. M. *Peter Pan*. New York: Tundra Books, 1988.

Blamires, Steve. *The Irish Celtic Magical Tradition*. London: Aquarian/Thorsons, 1992.

Bly, Robert. *Iron John*. New York: Addison-Wesley, 1990.

Brunton, Paul. *The Wisdom of the Overself*. York Beach, ME: Weiser, 1984.

Castaneda, Carlos. *The Teachings of Don Juan*. Berkeley: University of California Press, 1968.

_____. *The Power of Silence: Further Teachings of Don Juan*. New York: Penguin Books, 1988.

Chang, Garma C.C. *The Buddhist Teaching of Totality*. Pennsylvania State University Press, 1971.

Evans Wentz, W.Y. *The Fairy Faith in Celtic Countries*. Colin Smythe, Gerrards Cross, 1977 (Reprint).

Gimbutas, Marija. The Goddesses and Gods of Old Europe, 6500-3500 B.C. New York: Thames and Hudson, 1985.

Hope, Murry. *Practical Celtic Magic*. Wellingborough: Aquarian/Thorsons, 1987.

Kindred Spirit Magazine. Interview with Arwyn Dreamwalker, *Kindred Spirit* No. 25.

Macleod, Fiona. *Poems and Dramas*. London: Heinemann, 1933.

_____. *Iona*. Edinborough: Floris Classics, 1991 (Reprint).

Murray, James A.H. *The Romance and Prophecies of Thomas of Erceldoune*. Felinfach: Llanerch Publications, 1991 (Reprint).

Starhawk. *The Spiral Dance*, Tenth Anniversary Edition. San Francisco: Harper, 1989.

Stewart, R. J. *Celtic Gods, Celtic Goddesses*. London: Blandford, 1990.

_____. *Earthlight*. Longmead: Element Books, 1992.

_____, editor. *Robert Kirk: Walker Between Worlds: A New Edition of The Secret Commonwealth of Elves, Fauns and Fairies*. Longmead: Element Books, 1990.

Strieber, Whitley. *Transformation: The Breakthrough Century*. London: Hutchinson, 1989.

Tansley, David. *The Raiment of Light*. London: Penguin/Arkana, 1988.

Tolstoy, Nikolai. *The Coming of the King*. London: Bantam Press, 1988.

Vallee, Jacques. *Dimensions: A Casebook of Alien Contact*. London: Souvenir Press, 1988.

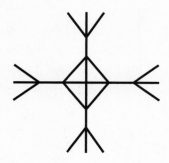

Index

LOOK FOR THE CRESCENT MOON

Llewellyn publishes hundreds of books on your favorite subjects! To get these exciting books, including the ones on the following pages, check your local bookstore or order them directly from Llewellyn.

ORDER BY PHONE

- Call toll-free within the U.S. and Canada, 1-800-THE MOON
- In Minnesota, call (612) 291-1970
- We accept VISA, MasterCard, and American Express

ORDER BY MAIL

- Send the full price of your order (MN residents add 7% sales tax) in U.S. funds, plus postage & handling to:

  Llewellyn Worldwide
  P.O. Box 64383, Dept. K483-9
  St. Paul, MN 55164–0383, U.S.A.

POSTAGE & HANDLING

(For the U.S., Canada, and Mexico)

- $4.00 for orders $15.00 and under
- $5.00 for orders over $15.00
- No charge for orders over $100.00

We ship UPS in the continental United States. We ship standard mail to P.O. boxes. Orders shipped to Alaska, Hawaii, The Virgin Islands, and Puerto Rico are sent first-class mail. Orders shipped to Canada and Mexico are sent surface mail.

International orders: Airmail—add freight equal to price of each book to the total price of order, plus $5.00 for each non-book item (audio tapes, etc.).

Surface mail—Add $1.00 per item.

Allow 4–6 weeks for delivery on all orders.
Postage and handling rates subject to change.

DISCOUNTS

We offer a 20% discount to group leaders or agents. You must order a minimum of 5 copies of the same book to get our special quantity price.

Visit our website at www.llewellyn.com for more information.

GLAMOURY
Magic of the Celtic Green World
Steve Blamires

Glamoury refers to an Irish Celtic magical tradition that is truly holistic, satisfying the needs of the practitioner on the physical, mental and spiritual levels. This guidebook offers practical exercises and modern versions of time-honored philosophies that will expand your potential into areas previously closed to you.

We have moved so far away from our ancestors' closeness to the Earth—the Green World—that we have nearly forgotten some very important truths about human nature that are still valid. *Glamoury* brings these truths to light so you can take your rightful place in the Green World. Live in tune with the seasons and gauge your inner growth in relation to the Green World around you.

The ancient Celts couched their wisdom in stories and legends. Today, intuitive people can learn much from these tales. *Glamoury* presents a system based on Irish Celtic mythology to guide you back to the harmony with life's cycles that our ancestors knew.

1-56718-069-8, 352 pp., 6 x 9, illus., softcover $16.95

CELTIC MYTH & MAGIC
Harness the Power of the Gods & Goddesses
Edain McCoy

Tap into the power of the Celtic goddesses, gods, heroes and heroines to aid your spiritual quests and magickal goals. *Celtic Myth & Magic* explains how to use ritual and pathworking to align yourself with the energy of these archetypes, whose images live within your psyche.

Celtic Myth & Magic begins with an overview of 49 types of Celtic Paganism followed today, then gives instructions for contacting the energy of the Celtic pantheon to channel it toward magickal and spiritual goals and into rituals. Three pathworkings will take you on an inner journey where you'll join with the archetypal images of Cuchulain, Queen Maeve and Merlin the Magician to bring their energies directly into your life. The last half of the book clearly details the energies of over 300 Celtic deities and mythic figures so you can contact the appropriate deity to attain a specific goal.

This inspiring, well-researched book will help solitary Pagans who seek to expand the boundaries of their practice to form working partnerships with the divine.

1-56718-661-0, 464 pp., 7 x 10, illus., softcover $19.95

All prices subject to change without notice

FAERY WICCA, BOOK ONE
Theory & Magick •
A Book of Shadows & Lights
Kisma K. Stepanich

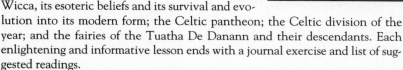

Many books have been written on Wicca, but never until now has there been a book on the tradition of Irish Faery Wicca. If you have been drawn to the kingdom of Faery and want to gain a comprehensive understanding of this old folk faith, *Faery Wicca* offers you a thorough apprenticeship in the beliefs, history and practice of this rich and fulfilling tradition.

First, you'll explore the Irish history of Faery Wicca, its esoteric beliefs and its survival and evolution into its modern form; the Celtic pantheon; the Celtic division of the year; and the fairies of the Tuatha De Danann and their descendants. Each enlightening and informative lesson ends with a journal exercise and list of suggested readings.

The second part of *Faery Wicca* describes in detail magickal applications of the basic material presented in the first half: Faery Wicca ceremonies and rituals; using magickal Faery tools, symbols and alphabets; creating sacred space; contacting and working with Faery allies; and guided visualizations and exercises suitable for beginners.

1–56718–694–7, 320 pp., 7 x 10, illus., softcover   **$17.50**

FAERY WICCA, BOOK TWO
The Shamanic Practices of the Cunning Arts
Kisma K. Stepanich

Faery Wicca, Book Two continues the studies undertaken in *Faery Wicca, Book One*, with a deepening focus on the tradition's shamanic practices, including energy work, the Body Temple, healing techniques and developing Second-Sight; meditation techniques; journeys into the Otherworld; contacting Faery Guardians, Allies, Guides and Companions; herbcraft and spellcasting; different forms of Faery divination; rites of passages; the four minor holidays; and a closing statement on the shamanic technique known as "remembering."

The Oral Faery Tradition's teachings are not about little winged creatures. They are about the primal earth and the power therein, the circles of existence, Ancient Gods, the ancestors and the continuum. *Faery Wicca, Book Two* is not a how-to book but a study that provides extensive background information and mystery teachings for novices and adepts alike.

1-56718-695-5, 320 pp., 7 x 10, illus., softcover   **$17.50**

All prices subject to change without notice

ISLE OF AVALON
Sacred Mysteries of Arthur & Glastonbury Tor
Nicholas Mann

Journey to a land where groves of ancient trees echo with the baying of hounds on a Wild Hunt ... where revolving castles, red dragons and bubbling cauldrons are intrinsic features of the landscape. This land is the Isle of Avalon—the magickal entrance to the ancient Underworld of the Celts. This book fully describes all aspects of this sacred site, based upon its incredible landscape, history, and mythology.

The ancient Celts, and the people before them, built an entire doctrine of death and rebirth around this mystical place. *Isle of Avalon* was written to restore the sense of the magical realm of the Otherworld to Western consciousness. It fully describes the physical and sacred topography of the British Isle of Avalon (pictured in beautiful photos) as well as its symbols, architecture, history, and accounts of visitation.

Journey to this magical place whose landscape resonates with the human heart, mind, and body to create a gateway to another dimension—and open a doorway to the eternal.

1-56718-459-6, 240 pp., 6 x 9, illus., softcover   **$14.95**

STRANGE ENCOUNTERS
UFOs, Aliens & Monsters Among Us
Curt Sutherly

UFOs and ghost lights ... sky quakes and strange disappearances ... phantom creatures and cryptozoological oddities ... all of these phenomena make us acutely aware of how little we really understand our world and the universe beyond. *Strange Encounters* was written by an experienced journalist and ufologist who has investigated many of the remarkable, yet true, events he documents in this collection.

Take a weird journey into the unexplained with 15 gripping stories gathered from the author's own journalistic investigations. From alien encounters to eyewitness disappearances to the Mars probe failure, these are puzzles without real solutions. But Curt Sutherly points out significant parallels between sightings in different parts of the United States, which add up to a pattern of strange occurrences—based on reliable sources—that cannot be intelligently dismissed. If you want the truth about these mysterious sightings and who's attempting to cover them up, then this book will engross you.

1-56718-699-8, 272 pp., mass market, softcover   **$5.99**

All prices subject to change without notice

ENCHANTMENT OF THE FAERIE REALM
Communicate with Nature Spirits & Elementals
Ted Andrews

Nothing fires the imagination more than the idea of faeries and elves. Folklore research reveals that people all over the world believe in rare creatures and magickal realms. This is a book with practical, in-depth methods for recognizing, contacting and working with the faerie world.

Enchantment of the Faerie Realm will help you to remember and realize that faeries and elves still dance in nature and in your heart. With a little patience, persistence and instruction, you will learn to recognize the presence of faeries, nature spirits, devas, elves and elementals. You will learn which you can connect with most easily. You will discover the best times and places for faerie approach. And you will develop a new respect and perception of the natural world. By opening to the hidden realms of life and their resources, you open your innate ability to work with energy and life at all levels.

0-87542-002-8, 240 pp., 6 x 9, illus., softcover $10.00

A WITCH'S GUIDE TO FAERY FOLK
Reclaiming Our Working Relationship with Invisible Helpers
Edain McCoy

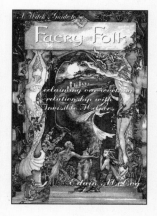

All over the world, from time immemorial, people have reported encounters with a race of tiny people who are neither human nor deity, who live both inside and outside of the solid human world. This book reclaims that lost heritage of working with faery folk that our Pagan ancestors took as a matter of course. Learn to work with and worship with faeries in a mutually beneficial way. Practice rituals and spells in which faeries can participate, and discover tips to help facilitate faery contact.

This book discusses the existence of the astral plane, the personality of various faery types and faery mythology. It even teaches you how to create your own thought-form faery beings.

Whether you are a Pagan or simply wish to venerate nature and commune with these creatures of the wild, *A Witch's Guide to Faery Folk* is an invaluable aid in this exciting exploration.

0-87542-733-2, 336 pp., 6 x 9, illus., softcover $12.95

All prices subject to change without notice

THE LLEWELLYN PRACTICAL GUIDE TO CREATIVE VISUALIZATION
For the Fulfillment of Your Desires
Denning & Phillips

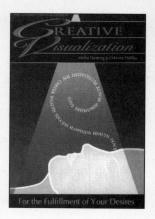

All things you will ever want must have their start in your mind. The average person uses very little of the full creative power that is his, potentially. It's like the power locked in the atom—it's all there, but you have to learn to release it and apply it constructively.

If you can see it in your Mind's Eye, you will have it! The power of the mind is not limited to, nor limited by, the material world. *Creative Visualization* enables us to reach beyond, into the invisible world of Astral and Spiritual Forces.

Through an easy series of step-by-step, progressive exercises, your mind is applied to bring desire into realization! Wealth, power, success, happiness, even psychic powers ... even what we call magickal power and spiritual attainment ... all can be yours. You can easily develop this completely natural power, and correctly apply it, for your immediate and practical benefit. Illustrated with unique, "puts-you-into-the-picture" visualization aids.

0-87542-183-0, 294 pp., 5 /4 x 8, illus., softcover   **$8.95**

CELTIC MAGIC
D. J. Conway

Many people, not all of Irish descent, have a great interest in the ancient Celts and the Celtic pantheon, and *Celtic Magic* is the map they need for exploring this ancient, fascinating magical culture.

Celtic Magic is for the reader who is either a beginner or intermediate in the field of magic. It provides an extensive "how-to" of practical spellworking. There are many books on the market dealing with the Celts and their beliefs, but none guide the reader to a practical application of magical knowledge for use in everyday life. There is also an in-depth discussion of Celtic deities and the Celtic way of life and worship, so that an intermediate practitioner can expand upon the spellwork to build a series of magical rituals. Presented in an easy-to-understand format, *Celtic Magic* is for anyone searching for new spells that can be worked immediately, without elaborate or rare materials, and with minimal time and preparation.

0-87542-136-9, 240 pp., mass market, illus., softcover   **$4.99**

All prices subject to change without notice